PRAISE FOR

DAMAGED
BUT NOT
DESTROYED

"Michael Todd is an innovative communicator with a passion to reach people for Christ. His new book will encourage and inspire you to remember that your failures do not define your future. No matter who you are or what's in your past, the Lord can forgive, redeem, and establish a new work in you! Even if you feel like you've messed up too badly—you can still be used by God. In fact, He has an even greater plan for your life than you could ever imagine!"

—ROBERT MORRIS, senior pastor of Gateway Church and bestselling author of *The Blessed Life, Beyond Blessed,* and *The God I Never Knew*

"The wisdom Mike exudes upon the pages of this book do not come from a place of theory; rather, they are the experiences amalgamated over time and seasoned with grace. *Damaged but Not Destroyed* encourages all of us and simultaneously leaves all of us with no excuse to play the victim."

—TIM ROSS, Upset the World, LLC

"Mike Todd has not simply written a book; he has created a blueprint to help us bounce back from whatever life throws at us. His transparency is transformative, inspiring, and sure to revolutionize your life. You may be damaged, but you won't be destroyed."

—DR. DHARIUS DANIELS, author of *Your Purpose Is Calling*

"Pastor Michael Todd once again has given us a true gift. *Damaged but Not Destroyed* should be in the hands of every person looking to redefine their past and allow it to fuel their future. There are few books that balance the dance of being both compassionate and challenging. This book will call you out of a holding pattern of excuses and launch you into the limitless possibilities of what's to come."

—PASTOR TRAVIS GREENE and DR. JACKIE GREENE,
pastors of Forward City Church

"In my brother Mike Todd's book *Damaged but Not Destroyed,* readers are invited on an exploration of faith, perseverance, and the transformative power of a personal relationship with our Lord and Savior. Mike's vulnerability and transparency is an inspiration to Christians everywhere and a mark of freedom to those who feel they are being held captive to the mistakes they've made. Redemption is available and free; Mike Todd's testimony throughout this book is proof of that. It is my honor and privilege to endorse *Damaged but Not Destroyed* and encourage every reader to get ready to be *transformed.*"

—KIRK FRANKLIN, Grammy-winning Gospel artist

DAMAGED
BUT NOT
DESTROYED

DAMAGED
BUT NOT
DESTROYED

FROM **TRAUMA** TO **TRIUMPH**

MICHAEL TODD

WATERBROOK

No book can replace the diagnostic expertise and medical advice of a trusted health care professional. Please be certain to consult with your provider before making any decisions that affect your health, including your mental health, particularly if you suffer from any condition or have any symptom that may require treatment.

Copyright © 2023 by Michael Todd

All rights reserved.

Published in the United States by WaterBrook, an imprint of Random House, a division of Penguin Random House LLC.

WATERBROOK and colophon are registered trademarks of Penguin Random House LLC.

Images on pages 16, 18, 19, 34, and 116: Gift boxes: imagedb.com; Shoes: Fotocam; Dart: RFedorenkov; Frames: Chief Design; all via stock.adobe.com

Hardback ISBN 978-0-593-44488-7
Ebook ISBN 978-0-593-44490-0

The Library of Congress catalog record is available at
https://lccn.loc.gov/2023002294.

Printed in the United States of America on acid-free paper

waterbrookmultnomah.com

2 4 6 8 9 7 5 3 1

FIRST EDITION

Most WaterBrook books are available at special quantity discounts for bulk purchase for premiums, fundraising, and corporate and educational needs by organizations, churches, and businesses. Special books or book excerpts also can be created to fit specific needs. For details, contact specialmarketscms@penguinrandomhouse.com.

This book is dedicated to my grandchildren. Because the Bible says "a good man leaves an inheritance to his children's children," I am making the decision to live my life H.O.T. (humble, open, and transparent), and to deal with my trauma so that you grandchildren will be able to be everything God calls you to be.

G-Dad loves you!

CONTENTS

DAMAGED
BUT NOT
DESTROYED

1

THE HIT YOU DIDN'T SEE COMING

Sucker Punched

The massive uppercut lands, and my head snaps back. Time slows, and I float to the mat, my too-short life passing before my dimmed and blurry eyes.

I see myself and my brother Gabriel suited and booted in matching fancy clothes. Gabe is just eighteen months older than me, and as small boys we got a lot of twin treatment. But as ten- and eleven-year-olds, that closeness is fading. Now we spend more time chewing each other out than twinning.

I see our family together just yesterday, joyful and laughing at the Tulsa State Fair. Gabe and I each won a set of boxing gloves emblazoned with American flags. We were so happy. Why couldn't we have stayed that way?

I see two brothers bickering and pestering until their mother can't stand one more minute. I see her help each of them tie on their boxing gloves and climb onto her bed, which magically morphs into a Vegas-sized boxing ring. Physical fighting is sternly discouraged in the Todd household, so this is extraordinary.

I see a microphone descend from the lighted catwalk (ceiling fan) above the ring and hear the announcer and referee (Mom) explain the rules:

1. No hits to the face.
2. No hits to the privates.
3. And . . . fight!

I hear the crowd roar and see myself, a frustrated baby brother whose time has come to shine. I'm quick and aggressive and more than ready to rumble, and I rain down blow after blow on Gabe's body: arms, chest, sides, even legs. Meanwhile, my brother—who is much bigger than me but also slower—stands motionless as a mountain, immobilized by the fury and speed of my attacks.

I hear the ref's whistle bring round one to a close, and I step back to catch my breath. I'm winning. I'm paying my tormentor back for everything. I'm going to absolutely destroy him! And I might want to be a professional boxer when I grow up, because, wow, I'm incredible at this.

"Mooooommmm!" Gabe wails. "He keeps hitting me!"

"Well," the ref replies, "try hitting him back. Now, fight!"

I see a menacing change in my brother's eyes. Something switches on, or maybe off. I see his arm wind up, like the Popeye cartoon on TV. I'm not sure what part of my body he intends to hit, so I'm waving my gloves all around my torso, trying to be there for the block.

The last thing I see before the lights go out is the American flag patch on his glove coming straight at my pretty face like a patriotic freight train. *Wait. Wha—*

Boom.

Right in the kisser.

TKO. (That's "technical knockout," for those who aren't into boxing or MMA.)

Ain't no hit like the one you don't see coming.

Sure, there are physical hits like the one I took from Gabe.

But mostly I'm talking about hurts that hit deeper—*much* deeper. Hits that don't heal with an ice pack. Hits that leave bruises on your soul. I'm talking about relational hits. Emotional hits. Ego hits. Financial hits. Family hits. And even spiritual hits.

Those hits—and how we can heal from them—are what this book is about.

But before we talk deep . . .

Allow Me to Introduce Myself

clears throat, in my best imitation of JAY-Z

My name is Mike.

My government name is Michael Alexander Todd. I'm the second oldest of five boys born and raised in Tulsa, Oklahoma, by two amazing parents, Tommy and Brenda Todd.

At the time I'm writing this book, my high school sweetheart, Natalie, and I have been married for twelve years. She is my good thing, the apple of my eye, the sugar in my Kool-Aid, the engine in my Ferrari (if I had a Ferrari), the best thing that ever happened to me, the finest woman to ever walk the earth, the wife of my youth (I'll stop there and leave the rest for *Relationship Goals: Part 2;* see below). Nat and I started dating when I was fifteen, which, now that I have children, is way too young. Out of our love, we have four incredible kids under the age of ten: Isabella Monét, MJ (Michael Jr.), Ava Rae, and Gia Joy.

When people ask what I do, I say, "It's complicated."

But if you want to hear it, here it go.

I'm a retired drummer and semi-accomplished music producer who ran sound at a church in the hood of North Tulsa, then got tricked into youth ministry and four years later was handed the church by the founding pastors, then watched our community of about three hundred mostly older African American church members snowball in a matter of a couple of years into a multiethnic, multigenerational, multiplying megachurch with influence around the world.

If that feels like a lot, it is.

But it's even more complicated than that.

In August 2017, I preached a sermon series called Relationship Goals that went viral. In the first message, I illustrated one of my points using Ping-Pong balls and water, and for some reason, two million people watched that clip within forty-eight hours. Two years later, I released my first book, *Relationship Goals: How to Win at Dating, Marriage, and Sex,* which went to number one on the *New York Times* bestseller list and has now sold almost a million copies. That's absolutely freaking crazy . . . until it happens, which is the theme of my second book, *Crazy Faith,* a handbook for doing extraordinary things with God based on what I've learned from my crazy journey with Transformation Church. It was also a *New York Times* bestseller.

But let me give you a little perspective. I dropped out of community college. (Shout-out to TCC! Nutrition 101 took me out.) All these crazy things happening to me? Nothing short of a miracle. For young Mike Todd, church and English class were the two most boring things in my world. God's funny, because now I'm both a pastor and a *New York Times* bestselling author. I'm proof that God uses foolish things to confound the wise. All of this is Him, y'all. And I'm so grateful.

But please don't get the impression that it's all fun and games and cash and fabulous prizes. The first time I ever saw stars and birdies circling my head was when Gabe's mighty uppercut connected with my ten-year-old jaw—but it was certainly not the last. I've been knocked to the metaphorical mat many times, and I fully expect to be hit again in the future. And most of the time, I probably won't see it coming.

I'm proof that God uses foolish things to confound the wise.

Have you ever been hit like that? Some of you are like, *Nah, this face is way too pretty to put it in harm's way.* I agree! You're beautiful. But I'm not talking about physical hits. Let me be H.O.T. (humble, open, and transparent) and tell you about a few of the hits I've taken over the years so we can get on the same wavelength.

The Dumb Hit

First let me tell you about a dumb hit. It's dumb because I did it to myself. As a young adult, I foolishly bought a luxury car that I could pay for but I couldn't afford. You know what I mean? I could *juuuuuust* manage the monthly payments, but I couldn't afford for anything to break.

Well, guess what happened. Something broke.

During the time my fancy car was in the shop, I let my insurance lapse. I mean, no one was driving it, so why pay for protection I didn't need? (It made perfect sense at the time to my still-developing early-twenties brain.)

After suffering through weeks without my precious ride, I finally got the call that she was ready to be picked up—on a day when Oklahoma winter was doing its thing and there was ice everywhere. I was *so* excited to finally get my car back, I decided not to wait for better weather. (This also made sense at the time.)

On my way home from the shop, I was ready to exit the highway when I saw a car spinning out ahead of me. By instinct I slammed on my brakes, which caused me to slide into the next lane. The car that was already occupying that lane smacked into me, and we both ended up on the side of the road. But when I started to get out so we could exchange information, that driver sped away on the icy shoulder to the exit.

It wasn't until I was climbing back into my beautiful, expensive car (which now needed even more repairs) that I realized I wasn't insured.

"Fifteen minutes could save you 15 percent or more" popped into my head. I called Geico right then and got insurance.

A couple of hours later, I called the claims department.

Taking my report, the claim adjuster asked, "Did you have insurance at the time of the accident?"

I answered, "My insurance was current on the day of the accident."

Yep. I lied.

And here's the thing: All lies are sin, but not all lies are a crime. That lie was a crime called insurance fraud, which was a felony.

It took five years for that lie to catch up with me, but it caught up with a vengeance. By the time all the paperwork and bureaucracy and hearings were done, I had mostly cleaned up my act and was a youth pastor.

Like, at a church.

Where parents and other parishioners and my boss (the senior pastor) expected me to be a role model for innocent and impressionable young people.

Mm-hmm. Yes. Of course it was *then* that I had to turn myself in at the local police precinct and be booked into jail—fingerprints and mugshots and the whole shebang. (My mugshot appeared the following week in our local edition of the *Busted* newspaper.)

I paid my fines and served my hours of community service and stood up in front of the whole church to confess. It was horrifying and humbling and dumb. It was a self-inflicted hit that caused damage far beyond itself. And, I'm sorry to say, it wasn't the only one.

Have you ever dealt yourself a hit? Maybe you knew better at the time, or maybe you didn't (I did), but either way, you're reaping the painful and/or humiliating rewards of self-inflicted damage. You're not alone.

The Distracted Hit

When I was fifteen years old, I was fortunate enough to meet the woman I would marry. That's right—Michael and Natalie sitting in a tree, K-I-S-S-I-N-G.

But I'm not gonna front: Happily ever after wasn't the whole story.

When I was seventeen, after Nat and I had been together for a couple of years, I started to get serious about my relationship with God. In trying to be sensitive to His Spirit, I felt like He was prompting me to spend more time with Him and less with everyone else. So I concluded I should break up with Natalie and focus on God. My girl was heartbroken, but because she also loved the Lord, she tried her best to be understanding and supportive.

I repaid that selfless sweetness by letting my eye get caught by another young lady. You can read the juicy, cringeworthy details in *Relationship Goals,* but long story short, I allowed my unchecked desires to fuel distraction. And distraction almost derailed my destiny! Y'all, I can't even imagine my life without Natalie Todd. But it almost happened, thanks to the hit I dealt myself with distraction.

Distractions have us looking the other way when we should be focused on where we're going. Has this happened to you? Perhaps you didn't see the hit coming, because your eyes were looking in the wrong direction.

The damage can permanently rearrange your face *and* your faith.

The Delayed Hit

Let's learn how to dive deep. Get your scuba gear ready.

When this kind of hit happens, we don't even feel it. It's what I've come to call a delayed hit: so ferocious that, in the moment, we're completely stunned because we don't have the capacity to deal with it or even the maturity to understand what has happened. In an instant, our growth is stunted.

I didn't realize I'd been hit until twenty-five years later. (More on that soon.) Sometimes we learn we've been hit when we find age-old debris buried in our behavior, coping mechanisms, and memories.

It's worth acknowledging that hits can be hard to talk about. We'd rather hide our hurts than travel back in time and deal with the difficult stuff. We prefer to put makeup on our mistakes. We want to edit our injuries and present a photo-shopped picture that doesn't show who and where we really are. But if you're human, you'll get hit. (Honestly, I'd be shocked if you haven't already been hit.) Pretending otherwise will stunt your growth and limit your greatness.

The Direct Hit

Are you one of those people (a) who believes somebody else when they tell you the stove is hot? Or are you the person (b) who has to touch it for yourself?

I need everybody to answer this one.

If you haven't already guessed it, I'm a solid (b). There are some things I've always known are bad and bad for me. But there was a time when I gave myself more credit than I deserved, believing I could cozy up to the heat because I was smarter, faster, and wiser, with enough common sense to get out before I got burned.

Well.

I was wrong.

The white-hot flame of perversion, lust, and temptation nearly burned me alive on the pyre of pornography. Instead of being in control of my thoughts and actions, I was a puppet to images, videos, and fantasies that directed my life and dictated my desires. It was like being a cup with the bottom knocked out, with no capacity to hold life-giving water. For years my partnership with pornography was a direct hit that left me completely empty with no possibility of fulfillment. Just a cycle of sin. Hit after hit after hit after hit after . . .

The Disaster Hit

Even if you've somehow managed to avoid all the previous hits (please tell me your secret!), I'm confident you've experienced what I call a disaster hit. It's a hit so big that you're not the only person knocked down by the punch. It affects entire communities, counties, countries, even continents. I'm talking about disasters like hurricanes, tsunamis, mass

shootings, tornadoes, wildfires, volcanic eruptions, even vi-
ruses.

The year 2020 delivered a right cross to the world that no
one saw coming. Covid-19 rearranged travel, business, education, government, family finances. It pretty much changed
everything. No one was unaffected.

That includes churches like the one I serve, Transformation
Church. There was no way we could have forecast that the
doors of our building would be shut for more than nine hundred days. We had to reimagine, reconstruct, and receive a
fresh vision for how we do church. It changed our team. It
changed our philosophy. It changed me.

When they happen, disasters make us feel like everything is
finished. Over. But together we've learned that disasters don't
last forever and God's grace will bring us through to the other
side, to a place we could never have imagined. But we had to
take the hit to find that out.

The Disguised Hit

If you want to talk about a hit that I could never have imagined, let's talk about the haymaker I took to the jaw from
success. I call it the disguised hit because it doesn't look like a
hit at all.

More money, they say. More influence, they say. Climb the
ladder. Boss up. Get to the top—fast. Fame! Fortune! Fran-
chise!

But nobody mentions how success can negatively affect
your family. How it can dilute your faith. How it can blur
your focus. How it can erode your foundation and jeopardize
your future.

There's nothing inherently wrong with success, but where

do you get your definition? What—or, better yet, who—is your source for defining success?

I found out the hard way that success fueled by the wrong source is just stress. (We'll talk more about this in a later chapter.)

The Domino Hit

A delusion is a false belief that is resistant to reason or confrontation with fact, and—let's be honest—we all get intimately acquainted with delusion and denial at some point in our lives. Unfortunately, I indulged in delusion at a moment when my family needed me to be clear-eyed and honest about reality.

It was right about the time that word started to get around about how God was blessing and multiplying my leadership at Transformation Church. I was getting invitations to speak not only around the country but also around the world. I was a featured guest on television, podcasts, and the radio and had just signed a book contract with a major publisher.

At the same time all that exciting stuff was happening, my wife started to express concern that our son, Michael Alexander Todd Jr. (we call him MJ), kept missing the developmental milestones that his big sister, Bella, had hit like clockwork. He wasn't responsive and interactive in the same way, and Natalie saw more red flags with each passing day.

I wasn't as concerned. Red flags? What red flags?

There was no way this strong and healthy boy, with my name but his mom's good looks, was anything but perfect. "We shouldn't compare MJ with Bella," I said, "because girls and boys mature at different rates. Apples and oranges. Give him time. He's probably just a late bloomer. Besides, look at all the ways God is pouring out blessing in this season! Let's not lose sight of what He's doing and get distracted by what-ifs. God is at work in a big way, and I can't believe He'd let that get derailed. Everything and everyone in Michael Todd Land is up and to the right. Up and to the right. Up and to the right."

But the day finally came when I could no longer deny that our beautiful boy was regressing instead of progressing. Eighteen-month-old MJ had stopped looking us in the eye, had stopped babbling and saying "Mama" and "Dada," was no longer paying attention to the people who loved him. He became fixated on random objects and got stuck in repetitive behaviors, then threw epic tantrums when we tried to redirect his attention.

Eventually I relented and agreed with Nat that we should have MJ's development tested. I'll never forget sitting in the specialist's office and hearing her say, "Your son is on the autism spectrum." I'm sure she was trying to be helpful and informative, but the level of detail about what MJ might face—inability to control bodily functions! total lack of verbal communication!—completely overwhelmed us. It felt like standing by with our hands tied as someone nailed his coffin shut.

We had barely any idea what autism was! We had never even heard the word *neurodivergent*. We didn't know any families who were dealing with it. And from the way the specialist described it, I felt like our boy was being handed a death sentence.

Natalie and I dealt with the hit of MJ's diagnosis in totally opposite ways. Nat's impulse was to get quiet, seek comfort, and find help. Sadly, for too long she didn't get any of those important things from me, because my impulse was to pray louder, work harder, and insist that everything was fine—or, at least, that it *would be* fine if we only had enough 𝕮𝖗𝖆𝖟𝖞 𝕱𝖆𝖎𝖙𝖍. Our God would send the right ministers, the right doctors, the right therapists if we spoke life, hope, and healing over MJ in faith. Everything would go back to normal.

Instead of comforting my devastated wife, I isolated her. Instead of empathy, I offered her blame. Instead of confronting reality, where God is always already at work, I resisted it. I didn't even want to acknowledge the hit.

MJ's diagnosis was what I call a domino hit, a knockout punch that begins an unstoppable chain reaction toward one of two places: hopelessness or healing. I got hit so hard, and there was no going back. I would fall either into a dungeon of despair or into the Healer's hands.

I am thankful beyond words that I fell (and am still falling) into Jesus. My domino hit sent me on a journey of truth-telling, self-discovery, empathy, intimacy, forgiveness, maturing faith, and increasing wholeness.

Maybe you don't know yet what your domino is, if it's already fallen or if it's teetering, ready to topple over with the slightest puff of wind. But at some point, there will be a hit you didn't see coming that knocks you flat and demands that you deal with it. Delusion and denial work only for a limited time.

I'm sorry. I hate to be the bearer of bad news. No, I really hate it. I'm a good-news guy, literally. To me, the bad news is worth mentioning only because the good news is so much better.

Reality is where God is always already at work.

The Covering, the Container, and the Contents

Let's do an exercise together. It relies heavily on your imagination. Now, I know some of you turned off your imagination in sixth grade and abandoned it as child's play. But I'm convinced that God gifted us our imaginations so we can catch His vision for our reality. So read this, and then close your physical eyes. I want you to see with your mind's eye: Imagine the most beautifully wrapped gift. The box is medium to large, big enough to fire up your curiosity about its contents. Could it be a new laptop? A designer handbag? Your favorite pair of shoes? Keys to a new Tesla? An all-expenses-paid ten-day trip to Tahiti and Bora Bora? Anything could be in there! Let your imagination run wild for a second.

Now stop reading. No, really. Actually visualize the gift for ten seconds. 10 . . . 9 . . . 8 . . . 7 . . .

Is your box heavy or light? (In my imagination, I can barely lift mine.) What color is it? (Mine is glossy black.) Go on—make it as pretty as you want. Something like this:

Maybe the wrapping screams *classy* (but in a subtle and understated way) or *fun* (with tons of color and ribbons). Either way, imagine that the wrapping was done by a professional, not by a parent, child, or significant other. The folds are too crisp and straight, and there isn't a fingerprint in sight. It's almost like you can't even see the tape! You find yourself staring at it and wondering, *How is this sculpted paper creation even held together?* There's a part of all of us that wants to leave something this perfect just the way it is, instead of ripping it open. But that would be dumb because then you'd never know what's inside.

Now imagine someone walks up to your perfect box, pulls out a Sharpie from their pocket, and starts casually doodling on the side of your gift. Nothing crazy, just their best cartoon version of you, with a big mustache. (If you already have a big mustache, don't worry. They also add a polka dot bow tie and a Flavor Flav–sized gold chain that says "Playa.") They're not trying to wreck it or anything, just adding some sizzle. Pretty soon they've filled up all four sides of the box, so they start creating a masterpiece on the top. Their sketches somehow morph from kittens and shapes to rants about their feelings and frustrations.

Let me point out: It's your box. You didn't ask for this. They didn't ask permission, but it's still happening.

Just as you're about to address their obvious violation, they take it even further. They pull out a baseball bat and begin to Barry Bonds your box. *Smack. Wham. Pow!* It's almost as if you're not even there.

The bat turns into a switchblade, and they start to carve. The switchblade turns into bleach, and one drop at a time, the once-saturated color fades. The bleach turns into a blowtorch, and by the time they're through, the bow is melted, the paper is mostly burned off, and the box itself is charred, smoking, and nearly shapeless.

Is your imagination working? Can you see it? The most

beautiful gift you've ever received seems to be nothing more than a smoldering pile of garbage.

What you're looking at is a visual representation of *damage*.

Let me be specific and personal: It's a visual representation of *my* damage. And I daresay this is a representation of *your* damage too.

Brokenness.

Insecurity.

Distorted self-image.

Fears.

Trauma.

Perversion.

Pain.

Failures.

Mistakes.

Disappointments.

Bad decisions.

Wrong relationships.

Ignorance.

Arrogance.

Every human being is made up of a mind, a body, and a

spirit. Think about your gift like this: The wrapping, or *covering,* is your mind; the box, or *container,* is your body; and the true gift, the *contents,* is your spirit.

Your relationships, circumstances, and choices inflict damage on your covering (mind) and on your container (body)— and whether you want it to or not, it affects your spirit. It's inevitable. Predictable. When it happens, many times it leaves you looking a mess. Your thoughts and feelings are fragmented and disorganized. Your physical, financial, and vocational health are limping along on life support. From the outside perspective, you look destroyed.

But I have good news for you: Your contents—what's inside, your true gift, your spirit—can't be destroyed by outside damage, because your spirit was handcrafted by God in His own image. Please hear me when I say this: No matter what happened to you, no matter who hurt you, no matter how hollow you may feel . . . I want you to know this.

The value is still in you. The priceless value that is laced through every strand of your DNA is still in you.

I want to clearly tell you something you may not have heard before: Your covering and your container may be beaten halfway to hell, but *nothing* you or anyone else can do

The value is still in you.

will ever lower the value of what God has put in you.

Take another look at that busted-up gift. If you were seeing it for the first time, would you even wonder what's inside? If you hadn't seen it *before* all the damage to its covering and container, would you even care about the contents? Probably not. In our consumer culture, we design packaging to communicate what's inside. We expect the covering and the container to reflect the value of the contents.

But that's not how God does it.

When He tells the prophet Samuel to visit the sons of Jesse to identify and anoint Israel's next king (1 Samuel 16), the prophet is surprised to find out that the boy God has in mind isn't the oldest, the strongest, or the best looking. "Don't judge by his appearance or height," God tells Samuel when the oldest son steps forward. "The LORD doesn't see things the way you see them. People judge by outward appearance, but the LORD looks at the heart" (verse 7). David is the youngest, smallest, and least impressive, just like many of us feel today: underqualified, underequipped, and overlooked. His packaging doesn't communicate "king" contents.

But David's Designer—God—knows what's inside him. The same way your Designer—God—knows what's inside you. He put it there. Get used to me saying it, because I'm going to say it a lot: The value is still in you.

You may feel like you'll never find love again.

You may feel like addiction will always control your life.

You may feel like the failure of your business defines your reputation.

You may feel like infertility has robbed you of identity.

You may feel like the college rejection letter determines your future.

You may feel like your success leaves no room for mistakes.

You may feel like raising kids alone will leave your family deficient.

You may feel like the public shame will haunt you for life.

You may feel like depression is going to debilitate you.

You may feel like anxiety is going to outlast you.

You may feel like your best days are behind you.

You may feel like abuse is inescapable.

You may feel like loneliness will never leave.

You may feel like money makes you and that you're only as good as your last deal.

You may feel like the pressure to perform will always be your prison.

You may feel like your hope is hopeless, your joy is jacked up, your faith is fading, and your love is leaking.

But find a mirror or switch on your phone camera, and tell yourself, "The value is still in you." This may be the most crazy-faith statement you've ever made, but it's true: *The value is still in you.* You are full of the King's contents.

That's right. I said it: You're full of it.

I'm writing *Damaged but Not Destroyed* because most of us have a hard time believing we have value, especially when our covering and container have been battered, cut, bleached, and torched. When you put this book down, I want you to be anchored in the truth, way down deep in your bones, that your contents—your spirit, your core, your eternal essence—were handcrafted with love and purpose by the Creator of the universe.

Your value is so significant that once you understand who

God has made you to be, you have the power to achieve victory in every circumstance. Your value is for victory.

But that's not even the craziest part.

God Can Use Your Damage

No, really. Read the heading again. The terrible, disgusting, painful crap that happens to us isn't all God-*caused*, but all of it can be God-*used*. He doesn't waste material. Our God is the ultimate upcycler, taking what anybody else would throw away and making art. "All things work together for good to those who love God, to those who are the called according to His purpose" (Romans 8:28, NKJV). He wants to use your damage—no matter how bad, how deep, or how ugly—to bring you into your destiny. He can and will use all the hits.

In this book, we're going to dive deep into the way God restores damaged people to His original design for the purpose of serving others and showing His glory on the earth.

It's an invitation to you—yes, *you*—to experience everything God planned for you even before He laid the foundation of the world (Ephesians 1:4). How do I know? Because I'm living it. But even more, I know because the truth is in His Word, the Bible.

I understand that many people reading this don't believe like I do. And that is completely okay. As a matter of fact, I love it. You can belong here before you believe. The principles in this book have the potential to transform your life no matter what you believe.

We're about to go on a journey of self-discovery and healing together, but first we've got to make a deal.

I, Michael Todd, promise to be H.O.T. (humble, open, and transparent) about my own damage.

Your turn.

I, _____, promise to be H.O.T. (humble, open, and transparent) about my own damage.

Now that we're on the same page, I commit to sharing the almost too real and raw truth about how my damage was inflicted and how God is healing me. Notice I said *healing*, not *healed*. I'm in process. This journey we're starting is about progression, not perfection.

I want to warn you that dealing with your past pain, your present problems, and the fight for your future will get messy. But it's so incredibly worth it. Stepping toward God is more important than staying the same.

Buckle up.

Get ready.

Let's go.

2

DANG, I'M DAMAGED

Damn-aged

Did this section's title catch you off guard? *Did the pastor just drop the d-word? Oh no, he didn't!*

Oh yes, I did.

Please hear me out. Let me tell you why.

If we're honest, when we've experienced real damage and it's as unrelenting as waves that pound against the shore—one failure after another, one regret after another, one rejection after another, one abuse after another—it leaves us feeling devastated. In other words, like we're damned: cursed to live in a perpetual cycle of hurt, harm, hopelessness, and hell.

I want you to know, if you're feeling like, "Damn, I'm damaged," I have felt like that too. Yes, a pastor. Yes, a "man of God." Yes, the man who believes in 𝕮𝕣𝕒𝕫𝕪 𝕱𝕒𝕚𝕥𝕙. I want to affirm you: Having that feeling is fair. God's okay with it. He's big enough to handle your real emotions. Jesus tells us, "In this world you will have trouble" (John 16:33, NIV). The thing about trouble is that it's usually traumatic. But the greater tragedy is un-dealt-with trauma.

If you're real enough to admit that you feel like, "Damn, I'm damaged"—because of the mistakes you've made, because of the goals you haven't reached, because of the violations you've endured, because you're still dealing with things you thought you'd be over by now—I want to let you know you're in good company.

Be encouraged: The current state of your damage does not determine the deliverance you can experience. And the guy we're about to meet is going to demonstrate how you can go from damage to destiny.

> The current state of your damage does not determine the deliverance you can experience.

Meet Phibs

If you've read any of the Old Testament—the Hebrew Scriptures, the Bible that Jesus read when He walked the earth—I'm sure you've discovered there are a bunch of people in there with long, unfamiliar names. For every Adam, Noah, Samuel, or David, there is a Methuselah, a Hazarmaveth, a Maher-shalal-hash-baz, or an Ammishaddai. (Tell the truth—did you sound those out or just skip over them?) We're going to get to know a dude with one of those long, unfamiliar names, a man who suffers more than his fair share of damage. His name is Mephibosheth, pronounced *muh-FIB-uh-SHETH* —but because I am me and I love to make God laugh, I call him Phibs.

Let me give you some background on Phibs before we dive in, because the context is what gives his story such incredible power.

It's true for us, too, right? Restoration involves God's Spirit helping us understand our own damage in a new way. His healing puts our damage in context so it becomes just one part, not the whole, of our story. No matter how damaged you are, your damage isn't all of you.

One of the main characters in Phibs's story is King David, the most famous, most beloved king of ancient Israel. You may already be familiar with some of his highlight reel. As a shrimpy shepherd boy who didn't get an invite to his own family's party, David becomes an unexpected warrior and uses a slingshot to kill a giant named Goliath (1 Samuel 17). As a gifted songwriter, he composes many of the lyrics found in the book of Psalms. As a middle-aged king, he catches sight of a bathing beauty who isn't his wife and has her husband killed so he can have Bathsheba all to himself (2 Samuel 11)—yet even after all that, God still considers him "a man after my own heart" (Acts 13:22; cf. 1 Samuel 13:14).

> No matter how damaged you are, your damage isn't all of you.

Now, I'm a movie lover and like to cast some of my favorite actors as Bible characters. It's in no way biblically accurate—let me make that clear! But making these ancient-but-true stories into a movie in my mind is one thing that helps me bring God's Word to life in my heart. So Dwayne "the Rock" Johnson is most definitely David in my version of this story. He's super strong, he's a little bit too good looking, and everybody—I mean everybody—likes him. They can't help themselves. Even people who don't want to like him like King "the Rock" David. And his few haters hate because everybody else likes him.

But before David becomes king, there is King Saul, the first monarch of Israel. On the big screen of my imagination, Saul is played by Samuel L. Jackson. Not Marvel or Star Wars or

Capital One "What's in your wallet?" Sam Jackson. Not Frozone from *The Incredibles* Sam Jackson. No, in my cinematic dreams, every role Sam L. has ever played in a Quentin Tarantino movie gets thrown into a blender to make my Saul menacing, dangerously unbalanced, and drunk on his own power. He didn't start out that way, but by the end of the king's life, when we first encounter Phibs, God has withdrawn His anointing (His approval and special blessing) from Saul and his descendants because the king is reckless, unstable, and utterly determined to go his own way.

Saul's son Jonathan, the would-be heir to Israel's throne, is played in my mind by the late, great Chadwick Boseman, the Black Panther himself. He's wise and brave, honorable and compassionate—definitely monarch material—but he's also determined to do things differently from his father. Prince T'Jonathan (of Israel, not Wakanda) can see that his dad, King Saul, is a loose cannon whose reign is going to come to an ugly, chaotic end. In fact, he knows that God has already reassigned His anointing from Saul to David and David's descendants. You might expect T'Jonathan to be mad about it— like, "*I* was s'posed to be king!"—but you'd be wrong. See, Jon and David have been best friends since the Goliath days. The Bible tells us that Jon loved his best bruh "as he loved himself" (1 Samuel 18:3) and that the two of them made a covenant (1 Samuel 20). Their bond goes even deeper than a son's allegiance to his father. Although T'Jonathan continues to fight for his dad against the nation's enemies, he also saves David's life on more than one occasion when Saul intends to kill him.

Those are some divided loyalties! That kind of family drama is bound to do some damage.

Prince T'Jonathan has a son named Mephibosheth. Every-

one calls him Phibs (at least in this flick). We meet Prince
Phibs, the king's grandson, when he's just five years old, on
the day when the royal household finds out that King Saul
and Prince Jonathan have both died in battle with Israel's
enemy, the Philistines. That's already a whole lot of damage
for one little kid, but look what else happens to Phibs:

> When the child's nurse heard the news [about Saul's and
> Jonathan's deaths], she picked him up and fled. But as
> she hurried away, she dropped him, and he became crip-
> pled. (2 Samuel 4:4)

Not only are his dad and grandad dead . . .
Not only is he no longer in the line of succession for the
throne . . .
Not only must he run for his life and hide out in fear . . .
But also, through no fault of his own, because of someone
else's mistake, Phibs is physically disabled for the rest of his
life.
People in that day and age would call him damaged.

When It's Not Your Fault

This is Mephibosheth's story: Before he is old enough to make
decisions for himself, he is damaged. In one day, his whole life
is turned upside down by circumstances outside his control.
He loses his father and his grandfather, he loses his home, he
loses his ability to walk, he loses his future, and he loses his
identity.

Phibs goes from being royalty to being on the run.

(I'm not generally a fan of spoilers, but in case you're worried: This isn't the end of Phibs's story. And it's not the end of yours.)

One way of studying the Bible is to look for types and shadows. It's a way of understanding people and events *before* Jesus, in the Old Testament, as foreshadowing the new kingdom life that would come *after* Jesus's death and resurrection and the arrival of the Holy Spirit. Mephibosheth was a real guy who experienced real events . . . but he is also a shadow of me. He is also a shadow of you. He foreshadows anybody who is damaged, and as we'll see in the chapters ahead, he shows us how the King heals our damage and restores us.

If we're clear-eyed and honest, many of us are to blame for aspects of our own damaged condition. We're reaping today the nonsense we sowed in our past— and I promise we'll talk a lot in this book about healing from that damage. But if you go back far enough in any of our stories, you'll most likely find damage that was inflicted by other people.

> If you go back far enough in any of our stories, you'll most likely find damage that was inflicted by other people.

Real Raw Warning

You remember in chapter 1 when I warned you I might get too real? One of my core convictions as a leader is never to teach or preach about something I haven't already gone through or am not currently going through. I think that keeps things authentic. So I've decided to model transparency for you right up front. This might be triggering for some who have experienced sexual trauma, and if you need to skip ahead, join us again at the next heading.

A few years ago, I preached a sermon series called Damaged Goods, in which I challenged our church to spend time in prayer and meditation, asking God to reveal the roots of our damage. During this time, I had a jarring experience: I remembered something that happened to me that had been lost for decades. At thirty-one years old, after having no conscious memory of this event, I was suddenly transported back through time twenty-five years. I remembered, clear as day, as if it had just happened. When I was a young, innocent, pure, naïve child of six or seven, my body was touched, fondled, and kissed by a neighborhood boy—and it was such a confusing and damaging event that my little-kid mind protected itself by forgetting. I had no clue, as a first or second grader, what sex was. But my mind couldn't cope with the chaotic mix of pleasure and shame, so it went into lockdown, and that trauma was thrown into a vault, chained up, and buried in the recesses of my soul. And the key was nowhere to be found. Until . . .

I was praying through one of my messages for the Damaged Goods series, asking the Spirit to initiate healing in other people's lives, and God decided to start answering that prayer with *me*. As I sat alone in Transformation Church's worship center one afternoon while the sound guy played music and tweaked some EQs, the Holy Spirit brought it all back to me. (Again, what I'm about to describe may be triggering for some.)

I remembered the neighborhood kid sleeping over at our house.

I remembered waking up and not understanding what he was doing.

I remembered being confused, both curious and afraid.

I remembered feeling ashamed and helpless to stop it.

I remembered acting like nothing happened and not telling another soul.

I was violated.

I was scared.

I was ashamed.

I was confused.

I was damaged.

Twenty-five years later, on a regular day, sitting there in the church that I led, with the Holy Spirit's help, I had one of the most powerfully illuminating experiences a damaged human can have: I remembered.

I got up, drove home in a daze, and told Natalie everything.

I think I've mentioned she is the best thing in my world, and here's another reason: She listened with careful attention and empathy to all the pain and shame and horror tumbling out of my mouth, and when I finally stuttered to a halt with tears in my eyes, she said with such grace, gentleness, and delicacy, "I am so sorry that happened to you. It wasn't your fault."

It wasn't your fault.

What Nat said to me then, I say to you now.

It wasn't your fault.

You didn't ask for it.

You didn't want it to happen.

They should have protected you.

It wasn't your fault.

It wasn't supposed to go that far.

You weren't okay with it.

You didn't know what to do.

It wasn't your fault.

You said no.

You did what you thought was best.

You didn't know any better.

It wasn't your fault.

Maybe you were young and innocent, and then an older relative, neighbor, or friend introduced you to sexual contact or content. It wasn't your fault.

Maybe you grew up in a prideful family that kept secrets to preserve their reputation, and you were punished for telling the truth. It wasn't your fault.

Maybe you were raised in a church environment where those in authority used control and manipulation to stay in power. It wasn't your fault.

Maybe the people who raised you inflicted or allowed verbal, physical, or sexual abuse instead of nurturing, protecting, and caring for you. It wasn't your fault.

Maybe you experienced a disaster or calamity that left you physically, mentally, or emotionally traumatized. It wasn't your fault.

Maybe you waited for sex until marriage only to struggle with infertility. It wasn't your fault.

Maybe you were faithful to your spouse only to discover they had an emotional affair. It wasn't your fault.

Maybe you never felt safe to be yourself. It wasn't your fault.

Maybe your family abandoned you. It wasn't your fault.

Maybe your dad was absent, and you never saw a tender, loving father. It wasn't your fault.

Maybe these four words are what your soul has been long-ing for. Maybe they've eluded you for decades. Maybe you've felt like you don't deserve them. But today I want to stand as a representative of God, your loving Father, and say, What-ever *it* was, I am so sorry it happened to you.

It wasn't your fault.

The Dartboard of Damage: What Hits and Sticks

Before we go any further, *breathe.*

Inhale . . .

Exhale . . .

Whoosah.

If you're still reading, I'm so proud of you. You're doing work that most people run away from, but this work is neces-sary to transform the trajectory of your life and legacy. Now that I've insisted that the damage wasn't your fault (it wasn't!), I also have to tell you that the pursuit of healing *is* your re-sponsibility. Let me tell you again: The damage isn't your fault, but it's now your responsibility. You may not be to blame for the original hit, but healing can't happen without you.

Let's define *damage.* We all get hit, but not every hit leaves a mark, right? So let's agree that what we're talking about when we talk about damage is *what hits and sticks,* like on a dartboard. If the dart bounces off or misses altogether, there's no damage. But if it's thrown at just the right angle from just the right distance with just the right velocity and force, *thonk.* Bull's-eye. You've got damage.

You're right: It's totally, completely, 100 percent not fair. It's okay to get mad. You're not crazy to wish things were different. But I have to tell you, with so much love: There ain't no amount of wishing that can take away the reality of what happened. Take however long you need to be angry, process, punch a punching bag, scream into a pillow, go for a long walk, and accept the profound unfairness of it all. Do whatever kind of self-care you need to do—praying, venting with a wise friend or family member, getting professional therapy (for me, it was all of the above)—because the fact that it shouldn't have happened doesn't change the fact that it did.

Fair or unfair, the damage is done.

God won't heal what you refuse to reveal.

To allow God to begin the healing process, we've got to acknowledge the hits that have left their mark on us. The first step is to take a thorough and honest inventory of the damage. Think about it this way: If you go to the doctor with a broken ankle and tell her you have a head cold, will you get the help you need most? No, because you didn't identify the real issue. You have to tell her where you are really hurt, where you took the hit.

In the same way, God won't heal what you refuse to reveal.

To help you visualize the types of hits that are most likely to stick, picture this:

If you don't know, I'm Black. Black people do a lot of things exceptionally well, but one thing I'd never heard about a Black person doing well—or at all, for that matter—is playing darts. So when God gave me this vivid mental picture of darts and a dartboard as an analogy for damage, I couldn't help but wonder, *Do Black people play darts?*

The answer is yes. And some of them play exceptionally well.

Deta Hedman is a Jamaican immigrant to England who picked up the sport as a teen and has been ranked as the world's number one female player several times. She was also the first woman ever to beat a male player in a televised major tournament. Ms. Hedman has two nicknames, both of which are bomb: "the Dark Destroyer" (which sounds like a pro wrestler) and "the Heart of Darts."*

I'm hype about that second one because it strikes me that many of us are damaged by the darts that hit our hearts (and stick!). If you're wondering what the darts are in this analogy, here are the four most common weapons that leave a mark:

- words: *messages that are spoken over us*
- actions: *things that are done to us*
- exposure: *contact with toxic content*
- environment: *a negative atmosphere or culture outside our control*

You've been dodging darts from birth. These are the aerodynamic weapons fashioned by your adversary (Ephesians

---

* "Deta Hedman: 'I Don't Really Think About How Many Titles I've Won, I Just Go with the Flow Really!,'" Love the Darts, July 11, 2016, https://lovethedartsmag.com/2016/07/11/deta-hedman-i-dont-really-think-about-how-many-titles-ive-won-i-just-go-with-the-flow-really; Becky Grey, "Deta Hedman: 'I'm Not Here to Please You. I'm Here to Play a Game That I Enjoy,'" BBC, August 13, 2020, www.bbc.com/sport/darts/53677651.

6:16) that are aimed at your purpose, whether you know it or not. From living rooms to classrooms, bedrooms to boardrooms, courtrooms to dorm rooms—everywhere we live our lives, darts are flying. Words, actions, exposure, and environment zero in on our covering (thoughts and feelings) or our container (physical, financial, vocational well-being) and poke holes in our wholeness. The place those weapons hit and stick is the domain, or the "where," of our damage.

We've got to tell the Great Physician where it hurts. Warning: Anytime a doctor starts examining where we're most broken, it gets uncomfortable. When God touches what's tender, the domain of our trauma, we may get triggered. But I promise you—here is where healing begins.

This is the dartboard of damage:

Let me explain how this simple game works. When a dart (word, action, exposure, or environment) flies, sometimes it hits and sticks in a domain. That's when it causes—you guessed it—damage. Hang with me as I explain the common domains of damage:

- **Disappointments** are circumstances that for reasons understood or unknown failed to meet your

expectations. Example: a parent not showing up for
graduation.

- **False teachings** are ideas and principles that were
  presented to you as fact but are not rooted in God's
  truth. Example: a child being taught racism.
- **Wrong choices** are decisions influenced by
  foolishness, clouded thinking, or strong emotion
  that have a negative impact on you or others.
  Example: drinking and driving.
- **Accelerated success** is sudden fame, increased
  influence, and/or a rapid rise in demand. Example:
  winning *American Idol.*
- **Ignorance** is a lack or denial of reliable information.
  Example: believing the earth is flat.
- **Unreasonable responsibility** is a heavy burden you
  adopted because of someone else's abandonment or
  your own assumption that you had to. Example: a
  son becoming "the man of the house" at a young
  age because of a parent's absence.
- **Scarcity** is the reality or fear of not having enough
  or of running out. Example: food shortage.
- **Abuse** is a violation or mistreatment by a person or
  system. Example: domestic violence.
- **Neglect** is a lack of care or nurturing attention.
  Example: a newborn being neglected by her caregivers.
- **Rejection** is being denied access or acceptance.
  Example: not being accepted to the college of your
  dreams.

Now that you understand the darts (the weapons of damage) and the domains (the where of damage), let's put it all
together and talk about the wound of damage.

The Equation of Damage

By a show of hands, how many people hate math? My hand is in the air, and I'm waving it like I just don't care. Let me be honest, though. I don't hate *all* math. I just hate it when they start throwing in letters, fractions, decimals, symbols, parentheses, etc. But simple math? I got that. So for anybody who shudders at the thought of being back in high school algebra, relax. We're keeping it basic. I promise.

Thinking back on my short-lived academic career, the main thing I despised about math class was every teacher's insistence that I show my work. If I got the right answer, why did it matter? But I came to learn that showing my work wasn't about pacifying the teacher; it was about understanding the pattern. When we understand the pattern, we can pinpoint the problem.

> When we understand the pattern, we can pinpoint the problem.

Learning this equation has radically changed my life and the lives of those around me. If you do your own work in this section, it will transform you too. This is what the equation of damage looks like:

$$dart + domain = damage$$

In other words:

$$the\ weapon + the\ where = the\ wound$$

Let me show you the work that some friends and I did one afternoon while editing this book. These are real people's real equations of real damage:

"You're stupid." + abuse = insecurity
(DART: WORD)   (DOMAIN)   (DAMAGE)

father leaving + rejection = fear of abandonment
(DART: ACTION)   (DOMAIN)   (DAMAGE)

finding porn + wrong choices = addiction
(DART: EXPOSURE)   (DOMAIN)   (DAMAGE)

toxic church + false teachings = hating God
(DART: ENVIRONMENT)   (DOMAIN)   (DAMAGE)

Are you starting to see how damage adds up? Here's Mephibosheth's equation of damage from his physical injury:

dropped as a child + neglect = shame, hopelessness, loss of identity
(DART: ACTION)   (DOMAIN)   (DAMAGE)

Here's my equation of damage from the unwanted encounter with the neighborhood boy:

premature sexual contact + abuse = perversion and shame
(DART: ACTION)   (DOMAIN)   (DAMAGE)

The intense shame and distorted thoughts and feelings I suffered throughout adolescence and even into adulthood were wounds—damage—that I sustained from somebody else's abusive sexual advances. I didn't *remember* the hit until much later, but the damage was real. My ideas about women, relationships, sex, friendship, the human body, pleasure, and so much more were perverted, and at the same time, I was nearly consumed by a cloud of condemnation. I had no idea if I'd ever see daylight again.

Perversion and shame weren't even the worst of it. As we'll explore in the next chapter, unhealed damage always drives us to throw some darts of our own—and I was no exception.

But before I jump too far ahead, it's your turn.

Math with Mike

Hello, class. Please sharpen your pencil because you're gonna need it. Now, don't worry. In Math with Mike, you get an A every time you do the work. Doing the work is the whole point.

As your teacher, I'm excited for you because as you commit to confronting areas of your life that carry damage, I know you're on the threshold of a life of wholeness, healing, and freedom. This is the life that you desire and that you deserve. God made you for this.

Before we do the hard work, let's ask for His help:

God, thank You for being here with me in this moment, to walk with me through the valley of vulnerability. Today I'm asking that You help me be humble, open, and transparent about the things that have hurt me and left a hole. I want to be whole, but I can't do it without the help of the Holy Spirit. Lead me into all truth. In Jesus's name, amen.

Hey, pro tip: After working these equations privately, check your work and your heart with a study buddy or your community. Doing this deep level of heart math on your own can add up to feeling overwhelmed. But this exercise is to help you overcome.

You may be asking yourself, *How do I get started?* Quiet yourself, find a comfortable spot, and use your imagination to go back and visit Little You.

1. **Remember** the first time you experienced disappointment, rejection, abuse, neglect, or one of the other domains of damage. (The full list is on pages 36–37.) What was the domain of your hit?
2. **Identify** what dart was used. Was it words? Was it an action? Exposure? A toxic environment?
3. **Explain** in a word or two how this wound shows up in your life today. This is the step where you have to be H.O.T. (humble, open, and transparent). Remember, God won't heal what you refuse to reveal.

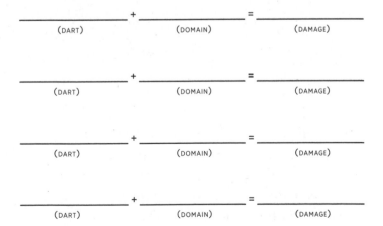

_____ + _____ = _____
(DART)   (DOMAIN)   (DAMAGE)

_____ + _____ = _____
(DART)   (DOMAIN)   (DAMAGE)

_____ + _____ = _____
(DART)   (DOMAIN)   (DAMAGE)

_____ + _____ = _____
(DART)   (DOMAIN)   (DAMAGE)

Don't stop now. There's more to explore. If you made it through these four equations and have lived longer than ten years, I challenge you to do four more in the back of this book. Dig deeper. Every seed of honesty you plant here will yield a harvest of wholeness and healing.

3

SAY MY NAME

My Damage Doesn't Define Me

When best bros Jonathan and David make their covenant, Jon extends their loyalty oaths beyond just the two of them to their descendants:

> May you treat me with the faithful love of the LORD as long as I live. But if I die, treat my family with this faithful love, even when the LORD destroys all your enemies from the face of the earth. (1 Samuel 20:14–15)

David doesn't forget, but because he relies on God's timing rather than his own, it's not until Mephibosheth is grown that David is fully in a position of authority to do something about that long-ago promise to his covenant brother:

> One day David asked, "Is anyone in Saul's family still alive—anyone to whom I can show kindness for Jonathan's sake?" He summoned a man named Ziba, who had been one of Saul's servants. "Are you Ziba?" the king asked.
>
> "Yes sir, I am," Ziba replied.
>
> The king then asked him, "Is anyone still alive from Saul's family? If so, I want to show God's kindness to them."

Ziba replied, "Yes, one of Jonathan's sons is still alive. He is crippled in both feet."

"Where is he?" the king asked.

"In Lo-debar," Ziba told him, "at the home of Makir son of Ammiel." (2 Samuel 9:1–4)

What jumps out at me first is this: Ziba identifies Mephibosheth not by his name but by his damage. Isn't that messed up? To be labeled with your pain and not your name. Besides being just plain rude, here's why that's significant: The Hebrew name *Mephibosheth* means "dispeller of shame."* So when Jonathan named his boy, I have to think his dream was that his son would never experience shame. Maybe fortune. Maybe fame. But definitely not shame, and definitely not because he is lame.

But this hater, Ziba, seems to think there is plenty for Jonathan's son to be ashamed of. Instead of calling him by the proud name given to him by his royal father, Ziba labels Phibs with his damage: "He is crippled in both feet."

My question is, Has this ever happened to you? Have you ever been labeled with your pain or predicament?

"I'm not saying she's a ho, but she's been around."

"I've never met anybody so petty."

"They should have graduated last year."

"That guy served time and can't get a job."

"She's such a perfectionist."

"She was raised in foster homes."

"He got kicked out of school."

"Their whole family struggles with *that*."

---

* "4648. Mephibosheth," Bible Hub, https://biblehub.com/hebrew/4648 .htm.

"This is their third miscarriage."

"Their business tanked."

"He can't talk right."

"She lived an 'alternative lifestyle.' "

"Their ministry never worked."

"He never lived up to his potential."

"She's always sick."

"He has three different baby mamas."

"His dad has the same addiction."

"She's already been divorced twice."

"They couldn't handle the pressure."

There will always be people who try to label you with your damage instead of calling you by your name. But I want to encourage you: Your name is powerful. Your name is unique. Your name has purpose attached to it. Your name is laced with identity. Your name has blessings connected to it. And above all that—God knows your name.

So my charge to you—when the Zibas in your life try to label you with a name that wasn't given by your Father—is to go back to 1999, turn up those Destiny's Child psalmists, and with boldness and conviction, tell all those Zibas: "Say my name, say my name." You don't have to answer to a name that wasn't given by your Father. Stop answering.

> You don't have to answer to a name that wasn't given by your Father.

You don't have to answer anymore to *addict, slut, felon,* or *failure.* You don't have to answer to *quitter, lazy, procrastinator,* or *inadequate.* You don't have to answer to *barren, broken, abused,* or *betrayed.* You don't have to answer to the damage that used to define you. When you're in Christ, He calls you by name. He says, "I call you My own. I give you My identity. My blood runs through your veins. You have purpose. You are enough. Your life has meaning. Your best days are in front of you. The value is still in you." (Check out the list of verses in the back of the book to see what the Bible says about your identity in Christ.)

No matter how damaged you are, your damage doesn't define you.

But . . .

If you *won't* allow God to heal you, to help you, to dig down deep and deal with it (whatever *it* is for you), damage can derail your destiny.

They Never Let Me Play

Before I was anything else, I was a drummer. My parents tell me that when I was eighteen months old, I'd take hangers from the dry cleaner, rip off the paper tubes, and use them as drumsticks. I'd waddle my way to the kitchen, plant myself behind a set of pots and pans, and start banging. Before long, the banging turned into beats, the pots turned into a pro drum kit, and the messy noise turned into music. By the time I was a teenager, I was playing multiple times a week for my parents' ministry team that traveled across the United States from church to church all summer long and for the youth band and children's events at our local church back home.

But man, if you'd asked me back then what I really wanted? The deepest desire of my heart? The thing I would do absolutely anything for? I wanted *so bad* to play drums on Sunday morning in "big church." (For those of you who aren't familiar with *big church*, it's a kid's way of referring to the main adult service of any congregation.) The regular drummer in big church was a mid-thirties dad named Chuck, and I knew I was at least as good as he was, maybe even better. So I convinced my mom and dad to take me and my sticks to adult choir rehearsal every Tuesday night. I'd get there early, smile at everyone, let them pinch my cheeks, and make sure my presence was known. Then I'd sit behind the drum kit in a maroon chair, using the chair beside me as a practice pad, waiting to be called off the bench and put in the game. I knew the music backward and forward. And I was ready—ready to show everybody what I could do.

> Not everything that appears good about your personality comes from a good place.

After the seventeenth time through "Power Belongs to God" (thanks, altos, for not knowing your part), I'd find myself watching Chuck play drums and wishing him dead. I know it's a little extreme. And I wish I were joking. I'd literally fantasize about Chuck slumping off the drum throne from a heart attack or malaria (I was fuzzy on the details) and see myself climbing over his lifeless body to take over the song without missing a beat.

But it never happened. (For the sake of Chuck and his family, I'm glad.) Sometimes, before and after rehearsal, I was invited to show what I could do, and I'd often get compliments and encouragement from Chuck, the music pastor, and the other musicians and choir members. "You're getting good, young man! Keep up the practice!" But the minute rehearsal started, I was banished to the maroon chair. They never let me play.

They said I was good, but they never let me play.

They applauded my commitment, but they never let me play.

They said I was talented, but they never let me play.

They said I had potential, but they never let me play.

I didn't realize it then, but their rejection was a domain of enormous pain—in other words, damage.

never let me play + rejection = obsession with greatness

(DART: ACTION)   (DOMAIN)   (DAMAGE)

It's possible, even probable, that there were perfectly legitimate reasons to keep my teenage butt at the kids' table. But the fact is, damage was done. Week after week, I was rejected. Month after month, that rejection turned to damage. Year after year, I unconsciously began to form my identity around the hit.

I remember the last time I sat in that maroon chair behind Chuck as he played the drums. This was the moment that transformed me into someone I had never been before. It was crystal clear to me that good wasn't good enough. I would have to be great. Nothing less than *great*. That night, leaving choir rehearsal for the very last time, I made an inner vow: *I will never be satisfied with being good. I need to be great.*

Some of us define ourselves by our damage and don't even notice.

How could I have known that my experience of rejection would shape so many of my future decisions and disappointments? It's impossible to acknowledge damage that we're not aware of—and it's especially hard to be aware of damage when we cope with it in a way that looks good from the outside. Unless you look closely, it doesn't look like damage at all.

Have you ever seen someone with incredible drive to succeed but that drive is their way of running from something?

> Our fruit is always connected to our root.

Have you ever seen someone who makes everybody laugh but the jokes are a cover to keep from crying?

Have you ever seen someone whose life looks perfect but something tells you it's an exhausting attempt to maintain control?

Please let me teach you from my experience. Not everything that appears good about your personality comes from a good place. If you're like me, your motivation may be rooted in rejection (*They never let me play!*). Or yours may be rooted in disappointment. Someone else's may be rooted in neglect. But it's imperative for each of us to discover the root of our motivation, because our fruit is always connected to our root.

We need to discover what drives us.

Check Engine

Let me ask you a question you may not know the answer to: What kind of engine is in the car you drive? *Uhhhhhhhhh . . .* is probably what most of you are thinking right now. A handful of car enthusiasts reading this probably know, but the majority of us don't care about the details as long as the engine gets us where we need to go. (Confession: I have no clue the type of engine that's been in any of my cars.) Car aficionados or not, there's one thing we can all agree on: Without an engine, there is no drive.

Now let me ask you a personal question: What kind of engine is driving your life?

Everybody copes with damage in different ways. Sometimes coping mechanisms are unhealthy straight out of the gate—like substances or habits to numb the pain or an overreliance on aggression to defend against abuse—but more often they are adaptations that seem to benefit us, at least for a while. That was the case for me. As a young man, I coped with the pain of rejection by driving myself to blow past good in pursuit of great. That's when I replaced my engine.

No downside, right?

Well.

Certainly a drive to be great has often helped me achieve beyond my own high expectations. The engine I unconsciously installed in my guts while glued to that maroon chair was loud and powerful. It was like the engine in one of those modded-out Subaru WRXs with the giant air intakes on the hood and high-octane flames blasting from a matched set of carbon-fiber exhaust pipes. For everybody who doesn't know what I just said—or care, for that matter: an engine you'd find in one of those *Fast and Furious* cars.

But I didn't know that there is a real cost to driving your soul (your mind, will, emotions) at a relentless 7,000 RPMs. That's too fast. That's unsafe. And it's liable to cause damage to the vehicle (that's you) and to others.

When damage is driving, there will always be a crash.

> When damage is driving, there will always be a crash.

Let me tell you about a few times when my damage did the driving.

For our wedding, Nat and I stayed up the whole night before (no exaggeration—the *entire* night) to hang little crystal balls from the light fixtures in the church to make them look like chandeliers (something we didn't have money to rent). My bride got half an hour of sleep the morning of our wedding because a good wedding wasn't good enough for me. We didn't eat dinner at our own reception because we were busy feeding four hundred people and making sure they had a *great* experience, and we didn't even have a first dance because we were too exhausted to attend the after-party. I look at our wedding pictures today and grieve. We could have had a good night's sleep, but hanging those crystals and appearing to have more money than we did was priority one. We could have enjoyed a good meal with each other and our family and friends, but impressing people was more important. We could have had a beautiful first dance, but good wasn't good enough.

I've sincerely apologized to my wife many times since then. But honestly, in that season, I didn't know what was driving me. However, now that I understand my wounds, I can see that when damage is behind the wheel, we're headed for trouble.

I'd love to say that was my only crash, but let's just say my damage has driven me time and time again. If my engine is rejection and I'm driven to be great (not just good), then everywhere I go, my damage *will* show up.

It showed up in high school when I ran for senior class president.

It showed up when God asked me to lay down my passion (music) to pick up my purpose (ministry).

It showed up when I became a father and my son had developmental delays.

It showed up when I led an organization and didn't have enough staff.

The ways we adapt to damage may seem beneficial on the surface. But at some point, we will discover that unhealed hits always become a hindrance in all ways. Always? Always, in all ways. Until then, whether we deny, suspect, or accept it, our damage is the driver—and not a good one either. The longer we're driven by damage, the more likely we are to end up in a ditch.

The Dashboard of Damage: Pop the Hood

For every one of us who is or has been driven by damage, here is some good news: When God designed you, He installed a dashboard with all kinds of lights and sounds to help you keep tabs on your valuable vehicle. (Because the value is still in you!) But much like your car's dashboard, it's useful only if you pay attention to it. If you ignore flashing lights and warning bells long enough, you become desensitized to the very indicators that are meant to keep you safe. There will come a point when you can't see or hear the warnings anymore—until the day you offer someone a ride and one of two things happens:

1. They stare at you in terror from the passenger seat, in fear for their life because of all the flashing lights and blaring alarms.
2. They tell you to pull over because there's no way

your vehicle will make it to the destination without harm.

In other words, our damage indicators are more evident in relationships. We're more likely to notice the check-engine light that's been blinking red for three months (or three years) when there's someone in the car with us.

> Our damage indicators are more evident in relationships.

Have you heard the saying "Hurt people hurt people"? It's true to some extent, but I think it's even more accurate to say, "Hurt people *who don't know they're hurt* hurt people." Every one of us is hurt. Damaged. But we don't have to stay on the highway and pretend everything's fine. Instead, we can pull over, pop the hood of our lives, and take a look at what's really going on in there. With routine maintenance at the hands of our Maker, we don't have to wreak havoc on the roads and run down innocent bystanders. We don't have to blow out a tire or blow up the engine going ninety on the interstate to keep up with culture. We don't have to be a danger to ourselves and those around us whom we're called to help. And the shift starts by paying better attention to our damage indicators.

Let's get acquainted with our God-designed dashboard. Check out the gauges below. Each dial shows a pair of opposite impulses, habits, or attitudes that indicate damage under the hood. When you're under pressure, where do you go? For example, do you go extreme, or do you get numb? When I'm under pressure, driven by my damage, I go hard to the extreme. No sleep, Red Bull, get everybody here, let's make it happen. My wife, on the other hand, when she's under pressure? Numb. Sleep and only sleep, hot tea, tell everybody to go away, only God knows what will happen. When we're driven by our damage, each of us goes toward one side or the other, and those indicators signal when we need a tune-up.

Keep in mind, these are *indicators,* not the damage itself. They point to the underlying damage that needs to be addressed by the Master Mechanic.

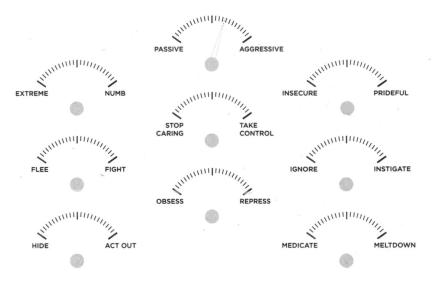

Damage pushes us to one side or the other on each gauge, but people who are progressing in their healing process aim for the midpoint on their dials. We'll call the midpoint "Health." Health doesn't mean you never overheat or get overwhelmed. Health is a growing ability to level out with the help of the Holy Spirit.

For instance, on the Insecure/Prideful gauge, I'd put myself somewhere between Prideful and Health since I naturally lean more toward pride than insecurity. (When I'm being driven by the damage I sustained back when they never let me play, the dial inches farther to the right.) Or, as another example, my Obsess/Repress indicator was pinned hard against Repress before the Spirit led me to remember the sexual abuse I experienced as a young child. Today I'm closer to Health because I've talked about it, I've gone to counseling, I have accountability in community, and I'm receiving healing through help.

Reflecting on your impulses, habits, and attitudes under pressure puts you, instead of your damage, back in the driver's seat. So, where do you go under pressure? Take a few minutes to get a look at your dashboard. Get quiet and breathe deeply. On each of the gauges on the facing page, draw your personal indicator. When your damage is driving and you're running under pressure, where do you go?

(Don't rush. I'll be right here when you get back.)

Good work. Now that you've taken a look at your dashboard, let me draw your attention to something I said a few sentences ago: *Today I'm closer to Health because I've talked about it, I've gone to counseling, I have accountability in community, and I'm receiving healing through help.*

Ooooohhhhhhh. That's a four-letter word we don't like: H-E-L-P.

> **Your healing is hidden in help.**

We think we should be able to get out of or around all our pain and predicaments alone. But God's Word tells us it's *not* good to be alone:

> Two are better than one,
>   because they have a good return
>   for their labor:
> If either of them falls down,
>   one can help the other up.
> But pity anyone who falls
>   and has no one to help them up.
>   (Ecclesiastes 4:9–10, NIV)

I need help. You need help. Say it with me:

I
need
help.

Help from the right people in the right context brings healing. James 5:16 says, "Confess your sins to each other and pray for each other so that you may be healed. The prayer of a righteous person is powerful and effective" (NIV).

Your healing is hidden in help. We'll unpack this later, but in the meantime, start opening up to the truth that asking for and receiving help are requirements for healing. You won't regret it. I promise.

4

DAMAGED AND STILL GOOD

Transferred or Transformed?

Before we turn from acknowledging our damage to the process of healing, let us give you a word of encouragement.

Natalie and I have been in intensive counseling for almost four years now. We are firm believers in theology *and* therapy. Some months ago, though, we came to a place where we both were weary and wanted to quit therapy, for a few reasons:

It's a lot of work.

It demands a lot of energy and investment.

It can be stressful.

And truthfully, sometimes we just don't want to talk about our issues.

I'm telling you this H.O.T. (humble, open, and transparent) information about us because, if you've made it this far in the book, you're doing heavy-lifting heart work alongside me—and by now you may feel about ready to throw in the towel or throw down this book. Don't do it! You've probably noticed it's a lot of work. It demands a lot of energy and investment. And man, it can definitely be stressful.

But you're doing it.

For real, *you're doing it!*

As we continue this journey together, know that I'm proud of you. Every step you take from here is a step toward the best version of you, toward a you that you haven't met yet but that you're going to love.

Let me tell you what our therapist told Nat and me when we were at the crossroads of giving up: *What you don't transform will be transferred.* Yikes! Let me say that again:

What
you
don't
transform
will
be
transferred.

Every step you take from here is a step toward the best version of you.

You've probably noticed, in working with your dartboard and dashboard to discern your damage, that at least some of your wounds were inflicted by your family . . . who were wounded by *their* family . . . who were wounded by *their* family . . . who were probably wounded by—you guessed it—*their* family. For many of us, looking closely at our family tree is like watching a never-ending rerun of dysfunction and damage. The cycles may not ever be talked about, but they are real.

We then pass our unhealed wounds on to our children. We can't help it. Generational cycles are a tragic statement of fact (Exodus 34:6–9). "The sins of the parents" shape us. Their unhealed damage turns into darts that end up poking holes in our wholeness.

I've made no secret of the fact that pornography addiction had a decade-long choke hold on my life. It started with the dart of seeing porn on a hotel room TV during a ministry trip (!) with my parents. Before I knew it, *The Flintstones* had turned into *Kinky Kong,* and I was stuck. I didn't think I could talk to anybody about it, so it became a secret that I hid in the dark.

Literally.

Every time it got dark, I found myself searching for ways to see X-rated images like that again.

A little while later but still before there were smartphones and wifi everywhere, my dad brought home a computer to help us kids with school. That's when I discovered you could find just about anything on this new thing called the internet (shout-out to everybody who remembers dial-up), which was the start of a much deeper plunge into perversion.

Nobody knew. I slept only three or four hours every night, trying to satisfy a thirst that could never be quenched in that way. But I kept trying, and that turned into many, many, many wrong choices, distorted perceptions of people, a loss of relationships, and—most damaging of all—sin.

Years later, when I began to walk in the truth, I had a man-to-man talk with my dad. I told him about some of the habits that were hindering my future, including my addiction to porn. Instead of scolding, punishing, or disowning me as I secretly feared, he told me a story.

When Dad was at Grambling State University, he traveled the world as a drum major in the world-famous HBCU marching band. On a trip to perform in New York City, he heard about a certain street where "everybody knew" you could make your erotic fantasies a reality. Let's just say it wasn't a street where you'd take a walk with your kids. Dad, who was then an early-twenties young man, decided to spend an evening on that street with, in his words, "a pocketful of quarters."

I laughed. "What on earth would you need quarters for?"

"The quarters were for the peep show, son." Apparently, you could walk up to a curtained storefront window and insert a quarter into a machine, and the curtains would pull back to reveal a nude young lady posing and dancing provocatively.

Dad didn't sleep at all that night. (Hmm, sounds like me in high school.)

When I heard that, I realized my dad had struggled, three decades earlier, with the same cycle of perversion I was trying to break out of. In the Todd family generational saga, it was the exact same scene, just a different setting.

As I began to share more of my struggle, my father stopped me and said, "I'm sorry, son."

My knee-jerk response was only, "For what? My choices are my own."

He disagreed firmly but with incredible compassion: "I should have dealt with this more aggressively and intentionally in myself so that you and your brothers wouldn't have to."

Did I mention I have four brothers? All five of my father's sons have dealt with this cycle of damage to some degree or another.

Because what isn't transformed will be transferred.

I know you may be tired of discerning your damage, but please hear me: The only thing worse than being damaged is allowing your damage to multiply in the lives of the people you love most. If you're tired of doing the work for yourself, consider the next generation of your family. Please don't pass your wounds on to the people who matter most to you.

Your healing isn't only for you. Toxic generational cycles are a real thing. But here's good news: Transformed generational cycles are a real thing too. What if you and I could be the pivot points for our entire family lines? I know that sounds too big for one person, but God's Word tells us that "a good man [or a good woman] leaves an inheritance to his children's children (Proverbs 13:22, NKJV).

> **Your decision for healing can change destinies.**

When most of us hear that scripture, we think of financial security and wealth. But what if the inheritance God is referring to also includes health? Emotional health. Spiritual health. Soul health. Communication health. Relational health. What if the work we're doing right now could result in a treasure of transformation for our family?

A fortune of flourishing.

Riches of restoration.

And a vault of value.

All I'm saying is that your decision for healing can change destinies.

We may have damage, and the work may be hard, but we decide whether we pass on to the next generation our damage or the good that's still inside. Let me show you what I mean.

Dented on the Outside

When I was growing up, my parents often struggled to make ends meet. Our family practiced **Crazy Faith** that God would provide for our needs, which meant we sometimes ate off-brand Fruity O's instead of Froot Loops. And forget about Pepsi—it was all about Shasta. One of the ways my mom pinched needed pennies was to shop the "dented and damaged" shelf in the grocery store.

Some of y'all are too bougie to know what that is, so let me explain.

I don't know if it's still a thing, but when I was a kid, it was a big thing. Grocery stockers would pull beat-up cans and packages with torn or missing labels from their regular spots around the store, toss them all together in a jumble (usually in the back near the bathrooms), and then drastically mark down the prices. They were discounted because of damage, almost begging people to take them home.

My brilliant mother, in addition to being a gifted preacher, is a wizard in the kitchen. A dented can? A torn label? A broken box? The more damage, the better. It was a challenge! She loved to show that something beautiful could come from something broken. Brenda Todd knew that even if the container was damaged, the value was still in there—and she was going to find it. She'd pile those raggedy-looking products into her cart, take them home, have her boys carry them inside, and then work her magic. When she was done, our family would sit around the table like we were in one of those heartwarming Hallmark scenes and feast on a meal that was *chef's kiss*.

Yes, those cans were damaged. But the contents were still good. The flavor was still there. The ingredients still had integrity. In my mother's masterful hands, what was once considered damaged became delicious. Not only that—the discounted contents also became a valuable blessing to the people who needed it most.

This is a picture of what God has planned for you. In the Master's hands, your bruises, breaks, and blemishes can become a blessing. I know it sounds crazy, but it is 100 percent true. The value is still in you!

And God will use your damage to accomplish your destiny.

That's why guilt, shame, and condemnation are so dumb. Ain't nobody got time for that. Whether the damage wasn't your fault or you are totally, completely, solely to blame—or, realistically, a little bit of both—drowning in shame isn't what God wants for you or from you. In fact, His Word makes this promise:

> There is no condemnation for those who belong to Christ Jesus. And because you belong to him, the power of the life-giving Spirit has freed you from the power of sin that leads to death. (Romans 8:1–2)

Jesus doesn't condemn you; He wants to rescue you! His death and resurrection make your freedom and healing possible. Yes, you're damaged. I'm damaged too. We all are. But if you belong to God in Christ, you're still good.

Today you can bring your damage to God. You can put your mess in the hands of the Master.

I have a direct question to ask you, my friend. Forgive me for being forward, but do you belong to Him? Have you given your life to Jesus? Have you offered Him your bruises, your bad decisions, and your brokenness? Are you trusting His masterful hands to make something life-giving out of

> **In the Master's hands, your bruises, breaks, and blemishes can become a blessing.**

your damaged life instead of trying to hold it all together yourself?

If the answer is no or you're unsure, right now I want to offer you the opportunity of a lifetime. The opportunity to experience redemption through repentance. Repentance is simple: It means "turn around." The way you've been living, the way you've been doing relationships—it's not working anyway. So repent. Turn around. Turn to God. He loves you. He wants you. He's waiting for you.

If you're ready to transfer your burdens to Him and be transformed into a brand-new creation, pray this simple prayer with me:

Dear God, today I surrender. I'm tired of doing life this way, and right now I'm giving You everything: all my failures, all my mistakes, all my pain, all my damage. From this point on, I belong to You. Thank You for sending Your Son, Jesus, as the payment for my sin. Today I'm putting my trust fully in Him. Because of the sacrifice of Jesus, His death and resurrection, my sin is defeated and destroyed. I no longer have to define my life by my damage. I repent. I turn. Today I am a new creation. I willingly invite You to be the Lord of my life. Send Your Holy Spirit to heal my mind, heart, and body. Renew my spirit until I look, live, and love like Jesus. Reveal Your purpose for me, and give me strength and courage to follow You wherever You lead me. Change me. Renew me. Transform me. I'm Yours. In Jesus's powerful name, amen.

If you just prayed this prayer, congratulations! You've made the best decision of your life. Your past is forgiven, your future is full of purpose, your eternity is secure, and your present is *so* valuable. This one decision, to put your life in the hands of our Master, has now given your damage meaning. It's only up from here—with the help of a faith community who will lift, support, and equip you for new life in Jesus. Don't sit on this; get connected to a church community *now*.

For all my friends who are now a part of God's family because of your trust in Jesus, I want you to make this declaration of 𝕮𝖗𝖆𝖟𝖞 𝕱𝖆𝖎𝖙𝖍:

Yes, I'm damaged. But because of Christ I'm still good.

The value is still in you—don't ever forget it; don't ever believe the lie again. And He who began a good work in you will be faithful to complete it (Philippians 1:6). God won't let any of your story go to waste. There is purpose in your pain.

Now it's time to start healing. Are you ready?

5

DAMAGED IS NOT (SUPPOSED TO BE) A DESTINATION

A Hopeless Place

My wife is great at many things: being an amazing wife and loving mother, being a caring and present friend, offering wise counsel—and man, she can cook. No, I mean . . . she can *cook* cook. One thing has eluded her genius, however. Nat is directionally challenged. At least once a week, no matter where I am in the world, I get a text message saying something like "I don't know where I am, and I have no idea how I got here. Mike, I'm stuck."

Every time, I think (only to myself), *How are you stuck? With all the technology in your car, how is it even possible for you to be lost?* She is wise in so many other ways, y'all, so without hesitation, I try to help her figure out where she is and then navigate to her intended destination.

I tell you this, which I hope she doesn't kill me for, to ask you, Have you ever been stuck in a place you didn't want to be and you weren't even sure how you got there?

This is where we find Mephibosheth: stuck in a place nobody would want to be.

When King David begins to look for Phibs, Ziba tells the king he's down and out in Lo-debar. There's another name loaded with meaning: *Lo-debar* means a place with no pasture.* That doesn't mean much to us city folks in the twenty-first century, but in a time when your wealth, security, and livelihood were based on land and livestock, you never wanted to find yourself in a place without good grazing land. "A place with no pasture" is a desolate place, a barren place, an isolated place, a place where life can't thrive. What I'm saying is, people go to a place with no pasture to die, not to live.

That's the place Mephibosheth is stuck.

Before we judge him too harshly, let's be honest with ourselves. Are there any places where you feel relationally desolate? Spiritually barren? Emotionally isolated? Financially dry? Is there any place that feels more like a grave than a garden? You very well may be in Lo-debar.

I think we can all agree that living in a parched place with no pasture causes immense pressure. Phibs's dashboard of damage is flashing red, and alarms are blaring, because he has responded to the pressure by hiding. He may also be numb, repressed, and/or medicated—Scripture doesn't really tell us his state of mind. What we do know is that he can't even afford his own place in Lo-debar.

> If you feel stuck, I want to let you know that you don't have to live in Lo-debar.

Imagine how much *that* sucks. He's gone from a palace to no place of his own, from royalty to no identity, from well to lame, from prominence to shame. And now, as Ziba is quick to point out, he's living off the charity of someone named

* "3810. Lo Debar," Bible Hub, https://biblehub.com/hebrew/3810.htm.

Makir, who could be a friend or even just a loyal Israelite citizen who wants to honor the legacy of Saul and Jonathan.

Can you see how Phibs must feel stuck? Not only is he crippled physically, but his surroundings also remind him every day that he's stuck in a place where nothing grows. If you feel like this, I want to let you know that you don't have to live in Lo-debar.

Phibs was five when he was damaged, and the Bible doesn't say exactly how long he's been in Lo-debar—but it's been decades. I wonder which year he stopped believing for healing. I wonder which week he stopped asking for help. I wonder which day he decided just to live with the hurt. I wonder which moment he lost hope.

> For anything in your life to change, you have to hope it can happen.

For anything in your life to change, you have to hope it can happen. The Bible tells us, "Hope deferred makes the heart sick" (Proverbs 13:12). Hopelessness holds you hostage in Lo-debar.

Before we go any further, I have to ask, Have you stopped hoping?

Have you stopped hoping you can escape that financial black hole?

Have you stopped hoping your family can be reunified and restored?

Have you stopped hoping you and your spouse can have a baby?

Have you stopped hoping your grim diagnosis is not the last word?

Have you stopped hoping you can learn to love yourself?

Have you stopped hoping you will work in purpose and make a living?

Have you stopped hoping your children will find salvation?

Have you stopped hoping you will finally quit your addiction?

If I were with you right now, I would grab you by the shoulders, look you straight in the eye, and say exactly what I'd say to Mephibosheth: Hope again.

I know you lost everything. Hope again.

I know you've tried before to reconcile and it didn't work. Hope again.

I know those miscarriages broke your heart. Hope again.

I know the doctor said there's nothing he can do. Hope again.

I know it's hard to believe you're worthy of love. Hope again.

I know low wages and zero benefits seem like your lot in life. Hope again.

I know it looks like your kids are paving brand-new roads to hell. Hope again.

I know you've never been able to permanently stop using. Hope again.

The reason hope is so powerful is that it's fuel for our faith. God's Word says, "Faith is the substance of things hoped for" (Hebrews 11:1, NKJV)—which means your faith is built by hope. So the most spiritual thing you can do, even if you're stuck and can't move out of Lo-debar on your own, is to hope.

You can hope your financial situation will turn around by this time next year.

You can hope family restoration will be your testimony.

You can hope to welcome a precious new life into your family.

You can hope your body's recovery will surprise even the doctor.

You can hope God will reveal your worth to you.

You can hope for a career opportunity with meaning and blessing.

You can hope your children will find their way back to truth.

You can hope you'll be delivered from the addiction's control.

As I write this, I'm getting excited because I can feel somebody getting ignited with heavy hope. I'm talking about the kind of hope described in Romans 15:13: "May the God of hope fill you with all joy and peace as you trust in him, so that you may overflow with hope by the power of the Holy Spirit" (NIV).

He wants to fill you with hope.

He wants you to overflow with hope.

He wants you to live in hope.

> Hope has a name: Jesus.

He wants you to have heavy hope, heavy like an anchor. No matter the storm, no matter the waves, no matter the situation: Hope can hold you.

How do I know? Because hope has a name: Jesus. Jesus is our hope. Jesus is our rock. Jesus is our anchor. He tells you, "In this world you will have trouble. But take heart!"—or hope—"I have overcome the world" (John 16:33, NIV). When you put your hope in Jesus, Lo-debar isn't your destination. It's just one stop on the road to your destiny.

So the lies the Enemy tells you to tell yourself—*This is just the hand I was dealt. This is the way it's got to be. I guess this is what's meant for me*—reject them. Lo-debar is a detour, not your destination.

Pursued by the King

Imagine the king of a country, the president of a nation, the top boss, sitting high in his loft of responsibility and wealth, thinking about you. Usually, the head honcho thinking about a commoner, an average citizen, an ordinary worker, is cause for concern. I imagine Mephibosheth would agree. After all, in ancient times it was common for a new ruler to kill the entire family of the previous ruler, just to make sure there was nobody left to claim the throne—so Phibs would definitely want to stay in stealth mode.

But . . .

King David, the most powerful person in all of Israel at this time—with a litany of legislation to be reviewed, diplomatic responsibilities to manage, and the burden of a nation's well-being on his shoulders—decides to use his invaluable time and emotional energy to think about Mephibosheth. Not to kill him, but to show him kindness.

> *God* in all His God-ness has *you* in all your you-ness on His mind.

Phibs is on the king's mind.

I always read Scripture anticipating truth hidden in the text for me. It's like a lavish treasure buried in the sand. Another word for this is *revelation,* or revealed truth. When I read about King David thinking about Mephibosheth, I find types and shadows. Remember types and shadows? These are people and events in the Old Testament that point to Jesus and how He relates to us today. If Mephibosheth is a shadow of us and if King David is a shadow of Jesus, I have some real good news for you, my friend: You are on the King's mind.

Maybe you feel more paralyzed and purposeless than ever before. You are on the King's mind.

You may not have one red cent to your name and you're barely scraping by, thanks to friends or relatives who feel sorry for you. You are on the King's mind.

Are you trapped by a physical ailment, bound by your body's limitations? You are on the King's mind.

Or perhaps you're blocked by mental illness or unhealed emotional trauma, tricked into desolation by a broken mind that needs restoration and renewal. You are on the King's mind.

Wherever your Lo-debar is, whatever you're doing or *not* doing there, you are uppermost in the King of the universe's thoughts. In other words, you are on the King's mind.

Think about that! *God* in all His God-ness has *you* in all your you-ness on His mind. And that's not even the best part! He wants to show you kindness. He wants to heal you. He wants to free you from bondage. He wants to prosper you. He wants to help you.

King David has no ulterior motive in pursuing Phibs, the same way God has no ulterior motive in pursuing you. The king's pursuit gains him nothing but gives Mephibosheth everything. And if you're like Phibs, lying there helpless and hopeless in your metaphorical Lo-debar, it's almost impossible to believe you're on God's mind. I get it. But that doesn't make it less true.

The thing that's interesting about this story is that Mephibosheth's hurts have him in hiding. He's been on the run. I bet he thinks he's so far off the grid that no one can track him down. He might believe that, crushed under all his heavy layers of damage, he's beneath anybody's notice. He thinks he doesn't even show up on the radar.

But Phibs is being pursued by the king, and there ain't no hiding once the King decides to find you.

Do you really think you're safe from grace—the unearned, undeserved kindness and favor of God our King? Sorry to disappoint you! Our King has a tracking device of unconditional love on you. You can run, but you cannot hide—not even in Lo-debar. God is relentless, like in one of those Japanese horror movies where there's no way to escape the spirit who's haunting you. Just when you think you've given Him the slip, you turn around and He's all, "Boo."

On my own journey of faith, I've been stuck in the Lo-debar of pornography addiction, the Lo-debar of shame from car insurance fraud, the Lo-debar of isolation from friends who've left the ministry, the Lo-debar of obsession with greatness, and the Lo-debar of debt and financial insecurity. But in every dry, parched desert place I got stuck in, I can remember the moment I realized the King was pursuing me.

Here's just one example. When I was twenty, I was a mess. Nat and I weren't married yet, but we were having sex on the sly. I was also cheating on Natalie and having sex with another girl. My addiction to porn and illicit sex was in the driver's seat, and I felt ashamed, worthless, and helpless. I was stuck in Lo-debar and couldn't see a way out.

I vividly remember going to church with Nat one morning. We'd taken only two steps through the door when a minister onstage called our names and beckoned us to the front of the church: "I've got a word from the Lord for you two."

That was it. It was over. The gig was up. We were busted. We knew right then and there we were about to get read for filth in front of e'rybody. We were caught. God knew exactly what we were up to, and He was about to make an example of us by airing our dirty laundry in front of everybody (which, in that church, was a lot of people).

In every dry, parched desert place I got stuck in, I can remember the moment I realized the King was pursuing me.

I reached for Natalie's hand to comfort her, but she batted mine away and looked at me like, *Boy, please.* Shame was eating her up inside just like it was gnawing away at me.

Full of dread, we started slowly walking up to the front. The minister began to prophesy before we even got there, so eager to deliver God's message to us that she didn't even lower her voice.

As she began to talk, my mind didn't know what to do with what I heard. I was stunned because it wasn't doom. It wasn't shame. It wasn't condemnation. It was nothing less than the King announcing He was in pursuit of *me,* and I couldn't wrap my head around it.

I have a plan and a purpose for you, Michael and Natalie. You will be united in marriage, and through

your relationship I will heal and restore marriages
around the world. It will be glorious. You will go
through seasons of trial and sorrow, but they will refine
you and burn away everything that doesn't belong in
your union. Turn to Me, and I will heal you. My glory
will be manifest in your family.

I hadn't taken one step out of Lo-debar, y'all. And still the King came looking for me. In that moment I knew exactly how the psalmist felt when he asked, "Who am I that You are mindful of me?" (see Psalm 8:4).

The King is pursuing you. You're never beneath His notice. Your damage can never be heavy enough to hide you. Under your pain, under your shame, under your armor of religion and judgment, under your disappointment with yourself and other people, He knows who you are and the purpose for which He created you. And He'll never ever give up on you.

GPS

Phibs's disability makes it impossible for him to pretend he's not damaged. He can't swagger down to Jerusalem under his own power and play like everything's all good. Everything is *not* all good. He can't walk. His family connections are a source of shame instead of honor. He has nowhere to call home. He can't fix the physical, emotional, or mental damage that he has sustained from the wear and tear of years of shame—so if he's going to the king, he's going damaged. There isn't any other way for him to go.

For many of us, though, our damage isn't so obvious—which can tempt us to hide or pretend, instead of just laying it all out for the King to see. But God don't lie. God won't bless who you pretend to be, only who you really are. Or let me say it a different way: God won't bless where you pretend to be, only where you really are.

When Nat is lost, my first step in helping her find her way to where she needs to go is to identify where she is. Think about your phone's GPS. If you want directions, your phone needs to know your current location. At Transformation Church we are determined to be H.O.T. (humble, open, and transparent) because we can't follow God's Spirit where He wants to take us if we're hiding or pretending to be somewhere other than where we actually are. How can we move to the brand-new place He is preparing for us on Deliverance Drive or Blessing Boulevard if we don't first admit we're camped out on Liars' Lane or Seductive Street or Religious Road or Agnostic Avenue? Every one of us is damaged—and the sooner we admit it, the sooner God can get to work redeeming it all and using it for His purpose.

> God won't bless who you pretend to be, only who you really are.

Stay put, and give Him your current location. Don't try to move first and then turn on location services, as if you haven't been living rough under Broken Bridge. Just stay where you are.

No, I'm serious.

If you're in a raggedy tent on Poverty Place, stay there.

If you're trapped on Anxiety Alley or Depression Drive, stay there.

If you're sneaking out to Homosexuality Hotel, stay right there.

Stay exactly where you are, and give God your current location. Lay it all out for Him. Don't try to hide. Be H.O.T. (humble, open, and transparent), and trust Him for what's next. Trust that if anybody can airlift you out of your Lo-debar, it's the King.

There is a GPS tracker on you—your destiny, your purpose, your life. And the truth about God's Positioning System is this: Where we are doesn't change who He is.

Carried to the King

King David couldn't care less what condition Phibs is in. He doesn't say, "Is there anyone in Saul's family still alive who has their act together? Who isn't super jacked up? I'm looking for someone decent who already quit smoking and drinking and chewing and stepping out and dating trash. Somebody who lives someplace respectable, with fertile pastures for their livestock and money in the bank."

No, even after hearing all the disgraceful details from Ziba, the king sends for Jonathan's precious yet damaged son (2 Samuel 9:5). David sends his people—could be servants, might be soldiers—down to Lo-debar to pick Phibs up and bring him in. In Phibs's case, "pick him up" is literal. Remember, the dude can't walk. Even if he wanted to, he couldn't get to the king by himself.

To anybody who feels stuck in Lo-debar: Yes, damage is caused *by* people. But that same damage is healed *through* people. For some reason, God chooses to use imperfect, damaged people to do His perfect work of restoration. So for any of you who have vowed never to let people close to you again or who believe you're better off by yourself, I submit to you that your healing is in someone else's hands. The King will send people into your life to carry you emotionally, spiritually, and even physically to a new place that you can't get to on your own.

But here's the tricky part: Your damage can skew your feelings and perspective about relationships, so your instinct may be to reject the very people whom the King sends.

The King sends help, but you may feel like it's another hit.

> Damage is caused *by* people. But that same damage is healed *through* people.

I can only imagine how Phibs must feel when the new king's royal security detail knocks on his door. Remember, back then, if the king's crew rolled up on you, it was pretty much guaranteed that your whole family was getting slaughtered. So when King David's clique shows up at the door with instructions to bring him in, Phibs thinks he knows what's coming. *I'm dead. It's over. The fat lady is singing at the top of her lungs.*

It's not crazy for him to believe he is next on the king's kill list. He's been hiding out for years, so he probably doesn't know that's *not* how the new king rolls (check out 2 Samuel 3–4). All he knows for sure is that his grandpa, the old king, put a bounty on the new king's head—and why would David be any different from Saul?

Let me say a word about the king's servants. Second Samuel doesn't tell us explicitly, but I think it's a safe bet that when David gives them their marching orders, not one of them complains about Lo-debar being too far or Mephibosheth being too damaged or David being too kind and merciful. They know this is the gig they signed up for: to carry out the will of the king.

This is the kind of servant our King calls each Jesus follower to be: ready, willing, and obedient to carry out His will. It's His will for us to rescue and restore damaged people. Remember "Hurt people hurt people"? It's also true that healed people heal people. Let me really blow your mind, though: *Damaged people (that's us!) can help heal people.*

Every phone call to express concern, every "just checking on you" text message, every shared tear, every milestone celebration, every challenging and encouraging conversation, and every time of prayer are the real-life, practical ways we carry damaged people to the King. That's the kind of servant *I* want to be. Let's not whine and cry about how hard it is to bring damaged people to the King, how long we've been on the journey with these people, and what we're giving up to help them.

> The King sends help, but you may feel like it's another hit.

Instead, let's be grateful for the servants who carried us when *we* were stuck and rejoice to do the same for others!

Let's flip the script just for a second and ask, Who are the Mephibosheths in your life? Seriously, take a moment and write down the names of three or four people who need your help, even in your damaged state, to get to the King. How can your story help their journey? How could your words wash their wounds? How might your presence be a gift to them? What will you do this week for each of them?

It's not fun or sexy to tell you my struggles and shortcomings. But if even a single person reading right now takes one step away from their damage and toward God's healing, it will all be worth it. That's the reason I'm writing this book.

Getting into the King's presence changes damaged people's present. And carrying them there is the greatest job in the world. I'm all in.

I want to be like the men we meet in Luke 5 who are so determined to carry their paralyzed friend to Jesus for healing that they give up the funk and tear the roof off the place where the Lord is teaching. If somebody needs to see Jesus, I don't want a stupid thing like my pride to stop me from clearing the way and tearing a hole in the roof to get them into the room. Sooner or later, I'll need someone to tear the roof off and lead me to the King too. Let me tell you about one of those times . . .

Not Just Another Sunday

Sunday. Game day. Go time. I woke up with a hundred thousand people on my mind, a hundred thousand who would show up to listen to my message. I prayed that I would speak only the words God wanted them to hear, though I tried *not* to think about how intimidating it is to speak on His behalf. People ask me, "Do you ever get nervous?" *Heck* yes. Every time.

In other words, January 16, 2022, felt like just another Sunday.

Before I go on, let me take a poll. I need you to be H.O.T. (humble, open, and transparent): By a show of hands, who thinks church is boring? Go ahead and raise your hand, wherever you are right now—in the coffee shop, on your lunch break, with your small group, at your cubicle, at the park, at the gym, in your bed—if you've ever yawned or dozed off during church. Confess now or forever hold your peace. Don't be shy, now. I see those hundreds of thousands of hands, and I'm in my office with both hands up. I went to church at least two times a week, every week, for my entire childhood, and to be real? I can't remember much of anything that was said or that captured my attention.

You, too, huh? Yeah, I get it. So when I started leading a church youth group, I was determined not to be the preacher whose voice rocked people to sleep and whose presentation was as bland as an old lullaby. I was determined to find ways to present the story of Jesus that would wake people up, get stuck in their heads, and drop down to their hearts, like that song that won't go away whether you want it to or not. (What's that song for you? For me it's "Baby shark, doot-doo, doot-doo-doot-doot." Did I mention I have four kids?)

For years I've used elaborate visual aids and surprising illustrations, all in the hope of creatively communicating the good news of the gospel. I've used lifting weights and treadmills. Golf balls, Ping-Pong balls, footballs, and basketballs. (I'm working on a creative way to use mothballs.) A boat floating on a water floor (inside a building). Windows and doors. High-end designer sneakers. On more than one occasion, fire. (It's my favorite.) Memorable, sometimes shocking, visual aids are kind of my thing.

Visual aids or not, I want to be effective every time I preach. But I always and especially want my first message each year to fly straight and hit hard—hard enough to stick. I want it to become an anchor for our families, our finances, our faith, and our future. My intention is to set vision and themes for the whole year, preparing people for what I believe God wants to do in and through our lives. So when I walked off Transformation Church's stage after preaching for two hours, one minute, and forty-four seconds (way longer than anybody expected), I had left my heart and soul out on the platform. I was soaked with sweat, high on adrenaline and the Holy Spirit, and hopeful that my delivery of the year's vision, "Here Is Holy," would paste itself to the minds and hearts of everyone listening as we faced 2022.

I wanted everybody to see God's vision for their life *clearly*.

Little did I know, things were about to get reeeeeeal blurry.

I got a few high fives, some tearful smiles of appreciation, and a ton of joy and pats on the back as I made my way to the office where my kids were waiting. Those four don't care how well or poorly I speak. They don't care what tools of biblical exegesis I employ to rightly interpret the Scriptures. They don't care whether my practical sermon applications are potent and timely.

What they cared about most on January 16, 2022, at 1:28 P.M. central standard time was sharing hugs and persuading me to get them slushies. What a perfect way to reset my priorities! Hugs and slushies with the #ToddSquad is one of the greatest ways I know to get grounded and gain perspective.

Plus, I knew hugs and slushies wouldn't even be the best part of my day. My wife and I had a forty-eight-hour "baecation" booked at a gorgeous hotel in downtown Tulsa starting that day, and I'd been looking forward to it all week. Two whole days of bae time? Yes, please. And thank you.

We ate together (slushies were involved); then Nat and I settled the kids with family and settled ourselves into our comfy room. Part of my regular practice in this season of growth is to be fully present wherever I am. *Here.* I've decided to live like *here* is holy. One of the practical ways I walk out this principle is the discipline of turning my cellphone off for twenty-four hours starting Sunday evening.

Phone off. Heart full. Bae by my side. I started to doze . . .

Nat sat up suddenly in the bed and asked, "Are you okay?"

I wiped the crust out of my eyes and blinked at her in confusion. "Yeah, I'm great. Are you?"

"Brie just texted and asked if you are okay, because a clip from today's message is the top story on TMZ." Brie is Nat's best friend and Transformation's executive pastor. We've been doing life and ministry together for more than a decade, and Nat and I both knew she wouldn't disrupt our Sabbath, or downtime, unless it was urgent.

I sat up, curious and excited. *Man, maybe someone at TMZ was touched by the love and hope I shared in the message and wanted to help get the word out!*

Nope.

I was about to find out this was not just another Sunday.

When Nasty Gets You in the News

I had a visual aid prepared that day to illustrate my message, "The Vision for Invasion," a little something I felt was simple but provocative. (I think I've mentioned I never want church to be boring.) My visual illustration was to smear spit on my baby brother, Brentom. Not just, like, a little spit. With as much drama and seventh-grader gross-out as I could find down deep inside (a lot), I hocked a serious loogie into my hands and slathered it on Brent's face.

It was absolutely disgusting. You could hear people in the room gasping, and some maybe even gagged a little bit—which is *exactly* what I was going for. I wanted people to feel repelled at a gut level, because sometimes the process of getting clear on God's vision for your life can get nasty. I wanted the audience to step into the Bible story, to hear and see what Jesus actually did according to Mark 8:23: "Jesus took the blind man by the hand and led him out of the village. Then, spitting on the man's eyes, he laid his hands on him."

That was the point of the illustration: that sometimes vision isn't sanitized, that we may feel like we want to pull back instead of lean in, that we think it shouldn't take getting our hands or anything else dirty. But if we want to see what God has destined for us, we've got to fight the gut instinct to run away when the situation gets nasty. And as far as I could tell in the moment, it worked exactly the way I intended. Brentom (who, as one of five Todd brothers, has both given and taken much worse over the years and who still regularly drinks from the same cup as me without permission, and I don't even get mad about it, much) was a willing participant in this example. As a matter of fact, we had done it twice before.

We did the spit thing, and then Brent cleaned himself up offstage while I wrapped up the message. He felt fine, I felt pretty good, and that was that. QuikTrip slushies, here we come, then off to our previously scheduled baecation.

Historically speaking, anytime something from Transformation Church has gone viral, it's always been good news. So now, late Sunday afternoon when I heard that a clip from the sermon had gone viral and was headlining TMZ, I thought, *Wonderful! Any chance to get the word out about Jesus is just fine with me.*

And then I saw the headlines.

- "Pastor Mike Rubs His Spit on Man's Face During Sermon."
- "Spit in Your Face Sunday."

- "When Salvation Becomes Salivation During a Pandemic."
- "Oklahoma Pastor Spits on Black Parishioner."
- "Saliva Sunday at Transformation Church."

They only got worse from there.

That minute and a half of gross-out, biblically reenacted brotherly love went around the world and back again in less than half the time.

And here's the thing: After watching the snippet that was getting shared on Twitter, Instagram, and Facebook, I couldn't help but agree with most people's reactions. On its own, with no context, no clue about my relationship with Brent, and no good, obvious reason that a self-respecting young Black man would allow himself to be spit on in public—there were implications of vileness that made *me* react with disgust . . . and I was there. I did it!

CNN and the other networks picked up the story. On Twitter, #MikeTodd and #Loogie started trending side by side. I was the top search on Google. The Shade Room, where Instagram goes for celebrity news and gossip, covered it with the opening line "Pastor Mike Todd nearly broke the internet."*

That's an exaggeration, but not by much.

Before the evening was half over, I was getting calls and texts from multiple time zones. By the next day, there were faith leaders and internet trolls, celebrities and influencers, denouncing me all over social media. People I considered

---

* Cassandra S., "Pastor Mike Todd Addresses Using Spit as a Demonstration Tactic in His Sermon," The Shade Room, January 17, 2022, https://theshaderoom.com/pastor-mike-todd-addresses-using-spit-as-a-demonstration-tactic-in-his-sermon.

friends distanced themselves and went silent. From the people who said a lot, to those who said nothing at all, the messages were deafening. I was overwhelmed by the attention and shocked that overnight I went from being valuable to being a villain in the eyes of so many people.

The spit had hit the fan. Being misunderstood sucks! Being misunderstood in public sucks even more. And being misunderstood in public in a way that could diminish how people (beloved of God) perceive Jesus—well, that sucks the most. The idea that I could get in the way of people coming to Jesus, even unintentionally, froze me at my core. I felt paralyzed. Couldn't take it back. Didn't know how to move forward. I meant to tear off the roof to bring people to Jesus, but instead, I needed somebody to carry *me* to the King.

> **Overnight I went from being valuable to being a villain.**

Three people—Natalie, Brie, and her husband, Aaron—did just that. We spent the next few days debriefing together. I cried, and they wept with me. In that safe place, I opened up about the confusion and hurt I felt. And their thoughtful questions and faithful presence helped me reset in God's presence. (In the coming chapters, I'll tell you more about the tools that helped me.)

Sometimes we are privileged to carry damaged people to the King. But in other seasons, we need the strong, gentle arms of the King's servants to lift us up and bring us into His presence. No matter how long or far you've walked, never be ashamed to ask for help on your journey to the King. Then look around to see who needs your help to come along.

6

PULL UP A CHAIR

To Heal or to Kill? That Is the Question

On May 19, 2022, a forty-five-year-old man named Michael Louis had surgery on his back. In the days following his release from the hospital, Mr. Louis called his surgeon's office a number of times seeking relief from severe pain. The surgeon saw him for a follow-up office visit on May 31, but according to his own written statement, Mr. Louis continued to blame the doctor for his ongoing pain.

On June 1, Mr. Louis drove to the hospital again, this time armed with a .40-caliber Smith & Wesson pistol and an AR15-style rifle, both legally purchased. He shot and killed the doctor who had performed his surgery, another doctor and office worker, and an elderly gentleman who had brought his wife for an appointment. And then Michael Louis shot and killed himself.*

To people who aren't lucky enough to live here, the multiple murders at Tulsa's Saint Francis Hospital were only the latest surge in a national wave of mass shootings. But Tulsa is

---

* Alexia Aston, "Timeline Related to Mass Shooting in Tulsa," *Tulsa World*, June 10, 2022, https://tulsaworld.com/news/local/timeline-related-to-mass-shooting-in-tulsa/article_3a362ef4-e2a5-11ec-b0bb-47b434a89395.html.

a medium-sized city that feels more like a close-knit neighborhood. Most of us Tulsans know someone whose life took a direct hit that day from Mr. Louis's rampage. Even if we didn't personally know a victim, we know family members who hugged a spouse or parent for the last time that morning. We know pastors offering what comfort they can to grieving relatives and friends, and hospital chaplains offering support to traumatized co-workers. We know anxious healthcare workers already stressed to the breaking point thanks to Covid who now say goodbye to their scared kids and head into work under even more strain.

> If we haven't yet started the process of healing, our words, actions, and attitudes will kill.

I don't know much about Michael Louis's life before his surgery, but if I were a betting man, I'd put good money on my hunch that he was burdened by unhealed damage. I'm not talking about his post-op pain, excruciating as it may have been; that suffering was just the latest dart life had thrown at him. I'm talking about unhealed damage from the past that crippled his ability to deal with present-day hits.

Hits happen. They just do. When hits happen, our response will be either life-giving or death-dealing—depending on whether we have begun the process of healing or not. Most of us, thank God, don't grab the nearest weapon and hold down the trigger when life's latest hit tries to take us out. But I promise, if we haven't yet started the process of healing, our words, actions, and attitudes will kill. They will kill relationships; they will kill opportunities; they will kill dreams; they will kill ideas; they will kill futures; they will kill purpose; they will kill legacy.

Unhealed damage creates a ripple effect in your life and in the people around you . . . *but so does healing.* That's why I want to give you a clear, step-by-step process that will prepare you to receive God's healing. In the next few chapters, we're going to take all the time we need to unpack and examine each of the five steps from different angles and in different lights, using my story and Mephibosheth's story as examples of the process in action. Before we click to expand, here's the thumbnail version:

1. Remember the hit.
2. Recognize the hurt.
3. Realize the hindrance.
4. Reset to humility.
5. Receive God's healing.

Let's start now with nobody's favorite: remembering the hit, the point of the pain, the site of the scar, the nerve of neglect, the root of regret, the location of loss. Why is it nobody's favorite? Because it will cost you your comfort.

1. Remember the Hit

Real healing can't happen in your comfort zone. Now, when I talk about remembering the hit, I don't merely mean recalling what happened. I want us to allow ourselves to sit with the truth, to really be present with the words, action, exposure, or environment that put a hole in our hearts. How?

Time to H.U.S.H.

All my life, I've been loud. I love to talk. In second grade, I was sent home with a note from my teacher, Ms. Robinson, that said, "He is a great student, but he talks too much." (It comes in handy now, Ms. Robinson.)

Another place where I got in trouble for talking a lot was in church. I can recall a particular morning when an elderly church usher watched me like a hawk during a service that was taking entirely too long. I had colored fourteen pages. I had eaten all the peppermints from the bottom of my mom's purse. I had examined the underside of the pew, built a fort out of hymnals, and folded offering envelopes into amazing, state-of-the-art jet planes.

The only thing left for me to do was to talk to the people around me and try to make them laugh. I don't know this usher's name (we were visiting another church), but she made a beeline for me across the sanctuary the very minute the service was over, extended two long fingers sheathed in pristine white gloves, and signaled for me to *come here.*

I walked sheepishly up to her tiny frame and whispered, "Yes, ma'am?"

"I been watching you all service," she growled, "and you, young man, need to learn how to hush."

Another "Yes, ma'am" was all I could muster, and I'm still elated that we never visited that church again.

I'll never forget how she said "hush."

I've been told to shut up, be quiet, keep it down, stop talking, zip it, close your mouth . . . but that was the first time I can ever remember being told to hush.

It wouldn't be the last.

Recall a few chapters back when I told you about the moment my obsession with greatness began? They never let thirteen-year-old Michael play drums in big church, and that hit of rejection smacked me right in the dartboard of damage and left a big, gaping hole.

Until a couple of years ago, I didn't know that moment was the moment I took the hit. In fact, if you had told me before then that much of my grown-up damage was the result of something that happened when I was thirteen, I would have laughed in your face and told you to move around. But that was before I learned how to H.U.S.H.: to Hear from God, Understand progressively, Share intimately, and get to the Heart of the matter.

> Hear
> Understand
> Share
> Heart

An elderly usher told me to hush the first time. But the Holy Spirit invited me to H.U.S.H. the second time. And now I invite you to do the same.

Okay, stop reading right now and listen. No, really. For the next fifteen seconds, I want you to put this book down, close your eyes, and intentionally listen to the sounds around you.

Welcome back. What did you hear?

For some it was the low hum of an air conditioner. For others it was the whoosh of cars speeding by on the highway. Many heard the indistinct murmur of the TV in the next room or the buzz of a mobile device. Some may have heard the annoying beep of a smoke detector in need of a fresh battery. Others let themselves hear their children screaming from the backyard (and instantly regretted it).

Hearing the truth of your inner experience is a choice.

A neurotypical brain is constantly filtering out sounds it doesn't think are important. Hearing what's going on around you is a choice. Something I didn't want to accept for a long, long time is that the same thing is true about what's going on *inside* you. Hearing the truth of your inner experience is a choice.

I've always been loud, big, flashy, and extra. I thrive on intensity. In fact, before I began the work of healing, I would create intensity when I felt like there wasn't enough. I would ramp up the drama and raise the stakes to *juuuuuuuuust* below everybody's breaking point and would love every minute of the adrenaline rush.

Natalie is the opposite. She thrives on peace, space, and quiet, which I used to routinely, thoughtlessly disrupt. A couple of years ago, she asked me, "Why are you like that?" And instead of getting defensive and angry—"Girl, why are you like *that*?"—I decided I actually wanted to know the answer. Why *was* I like that? It was a question that made me uncomfortable, but rather than running away from the discomfort, I decided to just kind of sit in it. With that one choice, my Flee/Fight gauge inched a little closer to the midpoint of Health.

Around the same time, I was reading an excellent book

called *The Ruthless Elimination of Hurry* by John Mark Comer, founding pastor of Bridgetown Church in Portland, Oregon. Comer argues in that book that regular silence and solitude are the most radical, countercultural spiritual practices we can engage in today. Maybe I don't need to say it, but up to that point, silence did *not* play a big part in my spiritual life—so between my wife and Comer's book, I had a lot to consider.

I began to dip my toe into being quiet. It felt foreign. Weird. Pointless. Dumb. Awkward. Difficult. I felt uneasy. *I'm just sitting here,* I would think, *doing absolutely nothing. This can't be helping.*

After about a week of (mostly uncomfortable) quiet time with God, my mind finally got quiet too. I ran out of thoughts to distract myself and ran into real silence. I could finally Hear. I could finally Hear Him. And I was ready to listen.

Throughout my journey with God, I've discovered a pattern in how He sometimes speaks to me: through pictures. As I sat there, finally silent enough to Hear, I got this picture of me spending time with my oversight pastor and mentor, Tim Ross. I can't explain how, but I knew it was a *right now* kind of thing. I needed to find out where Tim was and do everything in my power to get there.

I called him up, and he told me he was in Oklahoma City for a men's conference. I said, "Say less. I'm on my way." So I flew to OKC, carried Tim's Bible, assisted him for the day, and followed him everywhere he went. On the drive back to Tulsa, the two of us ended up in a Cracker Barrel outside the city. That was where I took my first little baby-faith step toward healing. That's where I remembered the hit.

We ordered breakfast, and then I relayed to Tim all that had been on my mind in the previous days—Natalie's ques-

tion, the practices of silence and solitude, leaning into discomfort, sensing that I was in some kind of transition but
feeling unsettled. He listened in-
tently and then asked, "When was
the first time you felt like good
wasn't good enough? Do you remember where you were when
you put in that engine, that drive?"
And then he turned his attention
to his humongous plate of eggs
and turkey sausage to give me
margin and time to Understand.
(See, Tim knows how to H.U.S.H.
too. Tim is a H.U.S.H. master.)

> You don't have to fully Understand to fully engage in remembering the hit.

Hearing from God happened in silence and solitude, which
brought me to a place where I could begin to Understand. I
like to call it Understanding progressively, rather than perfectly. You don't have to fully Understand to fully engage in
remembering the hit. Clear Understanding happens over time
and in stages, after a lot of thinking, feeling, and thinking
again.

Sitting there in Cracker Barrel, I got into the time machine
of my memory and began to jump backward. When was the
first time I felt this unrelenting drive to only ever be great?

Was the first time at twenty-seven, when I stayed up all
night before my installation as lead pastor of what would
eventually become Transformation Church, painting the walls
of the worship space, secretly hoping the new environment
would help people embrace me as the new leader? Nah, that
wasn't it.

Was it at twenty-one, when my loving mother "invited" me
to move out of the house (she kicked me out, y'all) and I con-

vinced two friends that an apartment wasn't practical for a drummer / music producer? We needed to be roommates in a four-bedroom house in an upper-middle-class neighborhood, and they should give me the master suite. Nope, that wasn't where the drive started.

Was it at seventeen, when NBA player and jazz bassist Wayman Tisdale invited me on tour while I was still in high school, which forced me to cram each week's schoolwork into Monday through Thursday so that I could fly out on Friday for concerts all weekend all over the world? Uh-uh, still further back.

Was it at fifteen, when I was chosen by our youth pastor to lead a gospel group of my peers that practiced twice a week for four hours at a time, with no pay but inspired by a vision and a drive to be excellent? Almost. We're getting close, but that wasn't it either.

> Faith begins where Understanding ends.

And then, like a ton of bricks, it hit me. . . . I remembered that freaking maroon chair in my childhood church and understood that I'd found the hit that, for the next two decades, was going to stick. (See chapter 3 for a refresher.)

Remembering made me feel anxious and vulnerable but also curious—so now, hearing Tim scrape his plate clean, I had a choice to make. Hide or heal? I decided to sit with my discomfort instead of shutting down. Rather than turning inward and withdrawing, I decided to do something I'd never done before, something that felt way too dangerous: I decided to Share.

I told Tim about that disappointing season of rejection when I was thirteen, and as he reflected with his words and facial expressions what he heard me saying, I was able to refine my Understanding.

Later, when I Shared with Natalie, I Understood even more with her insight, empathy, and reflection.

Hearing from God starts the process of remembering the hit, but I want you to see how Understanding and Sharing are a back-and-forth dynamic. When you take the risk to Share your hit, your damage, your brokenness, with a safe, trustworthy person or people, your Understanding progresses. It will always be imperfect because God is never done turning damage into destiny for your good (Genesis 50:20), but Understanding is about progression, not perfection.

Get wisdom.
And in all your getting, get understanding.
    (Proverbs 4:7, NKJV)

"Getting" is progressive; it's an ongoing action. It's something we continue to do. So if you're waiting to Understand everything about your trauma before you take a step on this healing journey, you may be stuck in the same spot forever. What you need is faith—I daresay 𝕮𝖗𝖆𝖟𝖞 𝕱𝖆𝖎𝖙𝖍—because faith begins where Understanding ends. What I'm encouraging you to do is take a step toward healing in faith, even if it's baby faith, maybe faith, wavy faith. (Sorry, y'all. I forgot what book I was writing. See *Crazy Faith* for details.)

> God is on a mission to rescue you.

Hear from God. Allow your Understanding to progress.

Share intimately in a safe space. Then you'll discover the real treasure, the Heart of the matter.

When I made the decision to H.U.S.H. and got quiet enough to Hear from God, His Spirit helped me Understand and Share the damaging hit I took at thirteen. I was able to peel back the layers of my Heart. My Heart had been hidden behind a relentless quest for greatness that caused chaos and exhausted me and the people around me. When I learned to H.U.S.H., God helped me excavate my Heart.

And that's when the real healing could begin. Remember, God won't heal what you refuse to reveal. Psalm 34:18 says, "The LORD is close to the brokenhearted; he rescues those whose spirits are crushed." Let me give you the passage remix: God is drawn to hurting hearts and scarred spirits. God leans close to tattered trust and insecurity issues. God longs to keep company with damaged people who are discouraged and dejected.

And though you may feel like you're drowning, He is on a mission to rescue you.

Imagine God running down the beach in slow motion like David Hasselhoff from *Baywatch*. (I may have just dated myself—scratch that.) Imagine God running down the beach in slow motion like Dwayne "the Rock" Johnson from *Baywatch*, looking to save everybody who can't keep their head above water.

This is our loving Father. He wants to save you.

I'm Outta the Hood, but the Hood Ain't Outta Me

I spent summer '96 in Shreveport, Louisiana, aka Ratchet City. My parents had gone on an extended ministry trip, so my brothers and I stayed with our relatives in the Boot. I remember crossing King Street in the Reisor neighborhood, back and forth between Grandma Leola's house and Aunt B's house, fascinated by the demeanor and attitude of the local kids my age.

Let's just say, some of my cousins and their friends had grown up differently from me and my brothers. We realized real quick we weren't hard. I'm not sure what had happened in those kids' lives—they might have come from very nice homes with plenty of love and consistent support. But from the outside looking in? It felt like they had grown up reeeeeeeeeeally rough.

I was only ten, but I knew early on that I would have to adapt to survive.

That summer, I went from polo shirts to sleeveless undershirts. I went from grammatically correct English to cussing you out in Ebonics. I went from Lunchables to Flamin' Hot Cheetos and pickles. I went from lighthearted jokes to ragging on people. I went from grocery store popsicles to freeze cups out of my grandma's deep freezer. I went from water bottles to drinking out of the hose.

Summer '96 was a summer of transformation.

By the time my parents came to pick us up, there was no doubt in anyone's mind that I had become a part of that hood.

Eight hours later, I was back in my regular quiet suburban Tulsa neighborhood, and to my surprise, none of the habits I'd picked up in Ratchet City translated as well as I'd thought they might. I found myself getting in trouble *a lot,* getting told on *a lot,* and suffering *a lot* of consequences for things I'd gotten away with a thousand times in the hood. But for some reason, I did *not* get away with them at home in Green Country.

As I sat, punished and contemplating yet another one of my poor decisions, I realized that acting wild was easier in the hood because my father wasn't there. His affirmation was absent; his wisdom was away. Not hearing the voice of my father led me to believe a lie about myself. The thing about my dad is that he was always telling me who I was. "Michael, you're a leader. You don't have to follow. You were born to do great things. You are creative. You are a man of character. You are a man of valor. You are respectful and respected. If you want to be like anybody, be like Jesus."

What I want you to take from summer '96 and apply to your life is that Hearing the Father's voice reminds us of our true identity. See, I had returned to Tulsa; I was out of the hood, but the hood wasn't out of me. It wasn't until I consistently heard my father's voice that I remembered who I really was.

My identity was tampered with in just a few weeks over one summer. Can you imagine how Mephibosheth must be tormented by lies? Because it's been decades since his father or a father figure has affirmed his true identity.

So when Phibs is carried out of his hood in Lo-debar and into David's throne room, I think he's suffering from an identity crisis. We're about to see that he's out of the hood but the hood isn't out of him. Listen to the way the king welcomes him:

"Don't be afraid!" David said. "I intend to show kindness to you because of my promise to your father, Jonathan. I will give you all the property that once belonged to your grandfather Saul, and you will eat here with me at the king's table!" (2 Samuel 9:7)

Whaaaaaaat? This sounds like a sweet deal to me! *Let me get this straight. You mean you're gonna be the plug and show me kindness, give me all my grandaddy's land, and let me eat with you at this buffet forever? Where do I sign up?*

That would be the typical response of someone who is healing. But Mephibosheth's unhealed damage doesn't respond; it reacts.

> Mephibosheth bowed respectfully and exclaimed, "Who is your servant, that you should show such kindness to a dead dog like me?" (verse 8)

Unhealed damage doesn't respond; it reacts.

Who talks about themselves like that? Oh, right. Someone who's damaged.

In case the "dead" part of that sentence isn't a dead giveaway, referring to himself as a dog shows us how Phibs views himself. Quick history lesson: Attitudes about dogs among ancient Jews were overwhelmingly negative. They associated our canine friends with violence, danger, and uncleanliness.* In their eyes, dogs weren't cuddly family companions; they were scavengers who spread disease.

Talk about low self-esteem, y'all. Phibs has it. He's dealing with shame, regret, comparison, self-condemnation. And the damage from all that stuff is *deep*. Like, way down deep. So deep that the king's kindness and generosity can't change the lies he believes about himself.

Phibs is out of Lo-debar, but Lo-debar isn't out of him.

You may be out of the abusive relationship, but insecurity isn't out of you.

---

* "Judaism and Dogs," My Jewish Learning, www.myjewishlearning .com/article/judaism-dogs.

You may not live in poverty anymore, but fear of lack isn't out of you.

You may not be on social media, but comparison isn't out of you.

You may not be cheating anymore, but lust isn't out of you.

You may not be in that church, but church hurt isn't out of you.

You may not work for that company anymore, but inadequacy isn't out of you.

You may have expanded your family through adoption, but grief isn't out of you.

You may have started giving, but greed isn't out of you.

You may have started counseling, but hiding isn't out of you.

You may be serving others, but pride isn't out of you.

You may be fine with being in the background, but envy isn't out of you.

You may manage your anger better, but rage isn't out of you.

You may have a good plan, but laziness isn't out of you.

You may have a team, but control isn't out of you.

You may have a lot of friends, but jealousy isn't out of you.

You may have the family you've always wanted, but loneliness isn't out of you.

You may be financially successful, but self-neglect isn't out of you.

You may be out of Lo-debar, but Lo-debar isn't out of you.

Here's my question for you: Is Lo-debar still in you?

If you're like me, I can already hear you saying, "But, Pastor Mike, it's been this way ever since I can remember. I can't escape these habits. You call it my old thinking, but it's my *only* thinking. It's sooo deep in me." I want to let you know, I feel you. What we're calling Lo-debar has just been life for many of us. If somebody makes us mad, we want to fight. If somebody hurts us, our cutoff game is strong. We're used to doing whatever makes us feel better in the moment: drink or pills or porn or shopping or golf or french fries—it doesn't matter. When we feel afraid or ashamed, we want to hide or run away or lie to protect ourselves. All we know is Lo-debar. And if we're willing to be honest, some of us have learned to love Lo-debar.

As someone who was stuck in Lo-debar, got saved out of Lo-debar, but still needed my mind to be renewed, I know it can seem like healing isn't possible. I'm here to tell you there's another way: You can be transformed by the renewing of your mind (Romans 12:2).

There's only one way to get Lo-debar out of you: Hearing from the King.

How does this happen?

Christian discipleship is a lifestyle of constants. There are some things about following Jesus and living in His Spirit that just don't change. Prayer is one of those things. Reading and memorizing Scripture is another. Why? Because when you talk to God, He wants to talk back—and one of the primary ways we Hear Him is through His Word.

God can certainly communicate with us directly, but here's how He speaks through Scripture: We read and study the Bible consistently to the point where it starts to become a part of us. Then one day our little ship of life starts getting rocked. The wind blows up out of nowhere, and the waves start crashing all around.

You get laid off.

Your husband starts acting crazy.

The check bounces.

A leader disappoints you.

You outrage the internet by wiping spit on your baby brother's face.

Boom.

That's when the anchor drops. God's Spirit calls to your mind what you've committed to memory—hidden in your heart—and that Word drops like an anchor for your soul. When you're tied to a sure and steady anchor, storms can't sink you. You just ride them out, maybe a little seasick but otherwise safe and secure. You can't be moved. Paul writes in his letter to the Christians in Rome, "Faith comes by hearing, and hearing by the word of God" (Romans 10:17, NKJV). So if you're not Hearing the Word on the regular, how will you have faith when it counts? You better start reading and memorizing what God, the King, says about you so that you don't believe the lies others say about you. You can Hear from Him.

Phibs's reaction to King David's words makes me think *in my best Chris Tucker voice* *he didn't hear the words that were coming out of his mouf!* The king wasn't just talking; the king was making promises. By my count, *three* promises.

1. I will show you kindness.
2. I will give you all your grandpa's property.
3. You will eat with me at the king's table.

In most Bible translations, David says, "You will *always* eat at my table." This isn't a onetime thing. It's a from-this-day-forward thing.

Here's what I believe, after meditating on this story off and on for years: Promise 3 is what makes it possible for Phibs to eventually believe promises 1 and 2. The king could show all the kindness in the world and grant all the land under his authority, but Jonathan's son is so damaged at this point that he wouldn't know what to do with any of it. Y'all already know how he reacts! He calls himself a dead dog.

Is your view of yourself so damaged that you can't accept what God says about you? I'm asking because that was me. I have always been and will continue to be H.O.T. (humble, open, and transparent) about my own season of living in a place with no pasture: addiction to pornography. You want to talk about shame, regret, and self-condemnation? Even after getting out of that prison of perversion, there was no way I could accept what God said about me—that I could be pure, that I could be faithful to one woman for the rest of my life, that I could lead a growing church and a worldwide transformation movement—until He got Lo-debar out of me.

> Is your view of yourself so damaged that you can't accept what God says about you?

Hearing from God on the regular allows me to experience transformation at the King's table of grace.

At the King's Table

Lo-debar has to be replaced, not just removed. Can I say that in a different way? Your old way of thinking has to be replaced, not just removed. So, in order to get Lo-debar out of you, you've got to get His kingdom into you. That's why promise 3—"You will eat with me at the king's table"—is the most important of the three. You won't have the ability to accept the King's mind-blowing kindness (promise 1) and over-the-top generosity (promise 2) until you live full-time in His presence, Hearing from Him (promise 3).

I'm being as literal and straightforward as I know how to be: Get in the King's presence. One way I do this is with something I like to call the Thirsty Thirty: ten minutes of reading the Bible, ten minutes of prayer, and ten minutes of worship daily. This is how you practically pull up a chair at His table and get in His presence so that you can Hear from Him.

You already know, progression over perfection. So start with five or seven minutes—whatever you can do right now—and then build up your faith muscles until it's twenty or thirty minutes or until you just get lost in intimate time with God. Read, meditate on, and memorize Scripture. Pray (that's just talking to God). Blast some worship music in your car, and sing at the top of your lungs, remembering what Christ has done for you (but please, keep your hands on the wheel, or pull over if you're about to have a Baptist fit).

Your old way of thinking has to be replaced, not just removed.

Or get quiet. You can Hear in His presence too. No matter how you do it, living in the King's presence will transform your perspective. As we'll see, this is exactly what happens to Phibs.

Use your holy imagination with me for a minute, and envision a long royal table covered in every kind of fancy food and drink you can think of. There are tall candles in elaborate gold candelabras, casting everything and everybody in a warm glow. It's light that everybody looks good in, the most flattering Instagram filter you've ever seen. You're at the table, dressed in your best tailor-made outfit, with a whole crowd of friends, family, acquaintances, socialites, athletes, influencers, movers, and shakers. As you look around the room, you realize you're seated at the same table with all these "important" people. You may feel a little out of place, but the seat has your name on it, so you stay and own the moment.

Now imagine yourself across the table from Mephibosheth. You wonder what he's feeling in this moment. Just twenty-four hours ago, he was a squatter in Makir's house, and now he has an assigned seat at the king's table, eye level with everyone around him. Nobody above him. He's on an equal level with everyone for the first time in his adult life. And on top of all that, maybe the most significant aspect is this: At this king's table, nobody judges him based on his damage. His atrophied, paralyzed legs have space in the grace of the king's table.

The king has enough grace for all the damage. Friend, I want you to know—no matter what hit you took, the damage it caused or is causing right now—you have a place at the King's table because that's what God's grace does. It gives you what you didn't earn, what you don't merit, in an overwhelming display of favor and kindness. Today Mephibosheth is sitting at the table of grace.

The same invitation is open to you.

The King invites you to gather as beloved friends and family around His table, to bask in the warm glow of His grace and favor, to receive and share every good gift He provides. He wants you to be so overwhelmed by His mercy that you're too grateful and satisfied to worry about anybody else's damage. You have an assigned seat at the King's table.

Remember promise 3? "You will always eat at my table." In other words, you will always be covered by grace. How long do you think it takes Phibs, eating every day in the place of grace, to stop feeling like a dead dog? If my own experience is any kind of model, it doesn't take long.

Today you may be in a situation that feels hopeless. Pull up a chair to the King's table of grace, and see how quickly the situation can change.

At this very moment you may feel trapped in depression and anxiety. Pull up a chair to the King's table of grace, and experience true freedom.

You may be in the middle of navigating the consequences of something you did wrong. Pull up a chair to the King's table of grace, and watch shame and condemnation fall away.

Or maybe you're on top of the world but still battling feelings of emptiness. Pull up a chair to the King's table of grace, and be filled to overflowing with the love of the King.

The King's Table

Instead of only picturing it in your mind's movie theater, let's create a visual aid you can come back to whenever you need a reminder of God's grace. In the space below, write down or sketch out what's weighing heaviest on your mind or heart right now—especially about yourself. Phibs felt like a dead dog. What do you feel like? Be specific and descriptive.

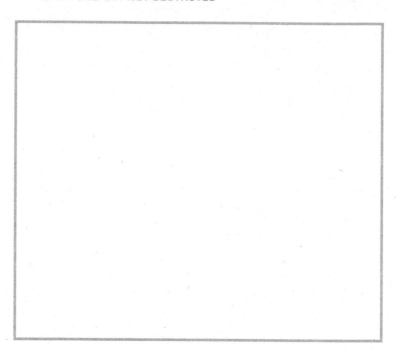

Remember, your Lo-debar—your old way of thinking—has to be replaced. To do that, turn to the back of the book (page 173), cut along the dotted lines of one of the boxes, and then tape your new rectangle cover over what you wrote or sketched just now. Decorate the clean cover with images, words, or verses of Scripture that remind you of God's endless grace.

Later today, or tomorrow, or next week, or a month from now when you need a reminder of the grace that is always and forever available to you, come back here to Hear from God. You can find an additional King's Table activity in the back of the book for future dead-dog feelings you need to get down on paper and allow God to cover with grace.

The table of grace is set for you. Pull up a chair.

7

SAY OUCH!

Height ≠ Healing

I'd never knock the Bible, because I believe it is the incorrupt-ible, infallible, reliable Word of God. But sometimes, if I'm honest, I wish there were a deluxe director's cut of the Scrip-tures that included all the in-between scenes that seem to have been edited out. I have so many questions.

How did Adam and Eve sew those leaves into the first biki-nis?

Did Noah ever get seasick?

What did Potiphar's wife do with Joseph's jacket?

Did Moses's feet ever hurt after all that mountain climb-ing? Don't tell me he didn't have at least one bunion.

How many times did Jesus turn water into wine at home for Mary before she told Him to do it at the wedding in Cana?

Did the little boy get some of the leftover fish and bread after the disciples stole his Lunchable to feed five thousand hangry people?

Questions. Important questions.

One thing I really wish I knew? I wish 2 Samuel would say what happens with Mephibosheth in the months and years after he starts joining the king at the table of grace. Because it's not as though all his problems are immediately solved, right? I mean,

Elevation doesn't guarantee rehabilitation.

the guy still can't walk. And his dead-dog mentality is a strong indicator that he's crippled emotionally and spiritually too. Damage like that doesn't just disappear overnight. Just because Phibs is elevated doesn't mean he's rehabilitated.

Does Phibs see the king's orthopedic surgeon? Consult with a physical therapist? Visit Jerusalem's top trauma-recovery specialist? Meet with the pastoral care team at the tabernacle?

Scripture doesn't elaborate, but from my own experience, pulling up a chair to Hear from the King is the beginning of the healing process, not the end. Remembering the hit is the first step, not the last.

1. Remember the hit. (Did that. Check.)
2. **Recognize the hurt. (It's time to do this.)**
3. Realize the hindrance.
4. Reset to humility.
5. Receive God's healing.

The loftiness of Mephibosheth's position doesn't mean he is healed. Elevation doesn't guarantee rehabilitation. As Deacon Drake says, "Started from the bottom, now we here."* But *here* doesn't mean "healed." This is true in every area of life. The new position doesn't mean renewed perspective. The corner office doesn't give you clarity of mind. The influx of followers doesn't equal fruitfulness. A different relationship doesn't ensure res-

---

* Drake, "Started from the Bottom," *Nothing Was the Same,* Cash Money Records, 2013.

toration. A large platform doesn't mean you're walking in purpose.

In fact, I can say with confidence that if you're not already on the road to healing, elevation will only increase the strain and pressure on the parts of you that are damaged.

Burdens feel heavier the higher you go.

A mountain climber will testify that the higher the altitude, the harder it is to breathe. Burdens feel heavier the higher you go. But we have a Savior who says,

> Come to me, all of you who are weary and carry heavy burdens, and I will give you rest. Take my yoke upon you. Let me teach you, because I am humble and gentle at heart, and you will find rest for your souls. For my yoke is easy to bear, and the burden I give you is light. (Matthew 11:28–30)

If we're going to exchange our heavy burdens for the Lord's light and easy yoke, we've got to actually recognize that our burdens exist. I'll be real with you: It's been only in the last two years that I've started learning how to do this.

2. Recognize the Hurt

You can say ouch.

Suck It Up, Buttercup

My brother Gabe was my first best friend. He's just eighteen months older than me, and from the minute we could both get around, we did everything together. We were partners: Gabe had ideas, and I did all the talking. (Did I mention I like to talk?)

It wasn't until we got to grade school at Hoover Elementary that I began to realize the reason I usually did the talking was that Gabe sometimes struggled to quickly communicate his thoughts. He had what they labeled a learning disability, and the school placed him in special classes to support his education. Over here, I was chatting up anybody who would listen, making friends left and right. But over there, Gabe didn't seem to have the same kinds of connections.

Then along came Derek. Freaking Derek, who was a bully and a butthole (and a child of God). Freaking Derek made fun of the way Gabe talked and did everything he could to humiliate my beloved big brother in front of others.

It made me so mad! I was furious on Gabe's behalf. But I was the *little* brother, so I let Gabe take the lead. I wanted my bro to grab Freaking Derek by his skinny neck, kick him you know where, and give him the stone-cold stunner. (We snuck and watched a *lot* of wrestling.) But at that time, Gabe wasn't confrontational at all. When Freaking Derek started in on him, he'd just say "Leave me alone" and walk the other way.

Day after day, week after week, month after month, I watched Freaking Derek rag on my brother—until one day I just couldn't take it anymore. I snapped. I knew the consequences of fighting with my fists would be severe, so I decided to fight with my words. I ripped him up. I let it fly. I dismantled Freaking Derek with every kind of insult and joke you can imagine. I ragged on his clothes. I ragged on his hair. I ragged on his shoes. I ragged on how little lotion he used. I ragged on his friends. To tell the truth, I ragged on his mama. Any cunning put-down that came into my mind went right out of my mouth without a second thought.

I can still see Freaking Derek's sad little face. I almost feel bad for him.

Almost.

Thanks to Derek and bullies like him, I learned early on that my words are powerful. But I also learned not to show weakness. I was damaged, because in fourth grade I closed the vault of my vulnerability. I reasoned that vulnerability gives the enemy ammunition. Like, if a shark smells your blood in the water, you are now bait. Sure, you may be hurt. But you better suck it up, Buttercup, and not show anybody.

Boys don't cry.

Be a man.

Shake it off.

Tough it out.

Get them before they get you.

You better not let them beat you.

Never let them see you sweat.

Nowadays we call this toxic masculinity, and I'll be a witness that *toxic* is exactly the right word.

That potion is polluted.

That tincture is tainted.

That drug is defiled.

I'm convinced that masculinity is necessary but it doesn't have to be malignant. We need to express emotions. Let me be more specific: *Men* need to express emotions. Let me be more inclusive: We all need to express emotions. Why? Because God designed feelings to come out, not to fester inside. If we lock them down instead of letting them out, our emotions will eat us alive from the inside out. Unexpressed emotions turn to dis-ease or disease.

If we don't outwardly express sadness, disappointment, and grief, they turn inward and fester into depression.

If we don't outwardly express fear, worry, and doubt, they turn inward and fester into anxiety.

If we don't outwardly express frustration, violation, and pain, they turn inward and fester into rage.

Science tells us that many physical sicknesses are linked to emotional illness.* If that's true, could our emotional healing be an antidote for our physical ailments?

I locked my vulnerability in a vault when I was really young. It's been only a few years since I found the combination, but opening up the door that I thought was protecting me has proved to be one of the most valuable gifts I could ever give myself. I started to use the power of words for healing.

> **Unexpressed emotions turn to dis-ease or disease.**

After that breakfast with Tim Ross at Cracker Barrel, when I remembered the hit—*They never let me play!*—I went home and got completely vulnerable with Natalie. It felt weird. It felt risky. I felt overexposed. I didn't just tell her about the maroon chair and wishing Chuck would fall off the drums to his death so I could play. In the safe and secure intimacy of our relationship, I admitted something that I'd never been vulnerable enough to tell anybody before: "It hurt. It really hurt. It hurt so bad that I did everything I could not to experience that hurt again. The rejection broke my heart. It hurt. It was painful. It hurt. Yeah, it was years ago. But it hurt."

* See, for example, "How Does Mental Health Affect Physical Health," WebMD, March 29, 2021, www.webmd.com/mental-health/how-does -mental-health-affect-physical-health.

I
said
ouch.

Ouch! That hurt!

This was a moment when I needed to H.U.S.H. I needed to Hear from God, Understand progressively, Share intimately, and get to the Heart of the matter. The Heart of the matter was that I was hurt.

And it took me just twenty-one years to admit it.

When was the last time you said ouch? Because it's only when you're vulnerable enough to admit you're hurt that you're vulnerable enough to get healed.

Recognizing the hurt, admitting where we're in pain, saying ouch is like taking a "before" picture. It's a snapshot of our current condition. My hope for you is that there will eventually be an "after" picture—after you've remembered the hit, after you've recognized the hurt, after you've received God's healing.

And I can't wait for you to compare and contrast where you've been with where God is taking you.

Your next step toward healing is to take a snapshot of your current condition. It's time to recognize the hurt. Don't freak out. Please don't try to cover up your scratches, dents, dings, and damage. C'mon, we're past that.

We need to be *real* for our "before" picture. No filter.

We need to take an inventory of everywhere it hurt.

> It's only when you're vulnerable enough to admit you're hurt that you're vulnerable enough to get healed.

Your "Before" Pictures

In the picture frames below, sketch or write about your emotional, mental, spiritual, and/or physical hurts from damage
in the past. Include the word *ouch* in at least one, because
sometimes you just have to say it.

Yes, recognizing where you're hurt is painful. This level of
self-awareness is hard, but I'm believing that your "after" picture is going to make all the work you're doing, with the help
of the Holy Spirit, so worth it.

When you recognize the hurt, you make space for grace.

(Once you start down this road to healing, you'll discover
hurts you weren't aware of. So we've included extra "before"
picture frames in the back of this book so you can say ouch as
many times as you need.)

The Ripple Effect

When the King's grace drops into your life, nothing stays the same. Just like when you toss a pebble into a lake, grace causes a ripple effect that starts with you and radiates outward to the lives of people around you.

When I've stood on the shore and launched a rock into the water, I've never seen where the ripple ends. Which makes me imagine, *Could it still be going? Could what I've done in a moment still be affecting things outside my view?*

Yes! That's what happens when grace drops in! Wave after wave of God's love, surge after surge of His blessings, a moment of mercy echoing throughout eternity. It's grace like a flood. The grace of God is *endless*.

But even more exciting, it's *available* to you and to me.

Here's some good news: God loves to drop His grace on people who don't think they deserve it. And let me be more frank: God loves to drop His grace on people *you* don't think deserve it. It's downright scandalous.

The sad thing is, a lot of damaged people believe God is out to get them, when God is actually out to save them. The gospel of Luke tells the story of a vertically challenged man named Zacchaeus—remember him? "A wee little man"—for those of us who grew up going to Bible camp, who wants to see Jesus. Zacchaeus is a tax collector, a Jewish man who is collaborating with the pagan Roman invaders to steal his neighbors' hard-earned money. Now remember, we're not talking about fairly elected officials and IRS accountants here. We're talking about a foreign army oppressing people, demanding however much money they feel like stealing today. And to collect all that taxation without representation, the Romans use Jewish people like Zacchaeus.

It's fair to say that greedy, treacherous, shiesty, damaged Zacky isn't everybody's favorite guy. Yet when he encounters Jesus, when grace drops unexpectedly into his life, Zac changes his priorities and pays back all the money he's ever stolen.

That's when Jesus says, "I came to ignore and reject the damaged."

Nah, I'm playing. Just making sure you're still awake.

This is what Jesus actually says: "[I] came to seek and save those who are lost" (Luke 19:10). Jesus comes to seek, find, and save those who are lost, frustrated, disappointed, wounded, depressed, poor, abandoned, anxious, traumatized, angry, and socially unacceptable.

Me.

You.

Us.

In Jesus, grace drops in and changes everything.

Zacchaeus experiences the ripple effect of grace, and it results in him repaying the people he ripped off . . . which changes their families . . . which changes the neighborhood . . . which changes the whole city. One man's encounter with grace changes an entire community.

That's so powerful.

Mephibosheth experiences the ripple effect of grace too. And for him, it looks like inheriting wealth and status intended for his father, Jonathan. Now Phibs will receive the undeserved, unearned favor and kindness of the king. Mephibosheth doesn't work for it. He receives it.

By grace you have been saved through faith, and that not of yourselves; it is the gift of God. (Ephesians 2:8, NKJV)

All I'm trying to say is, when grace drops in, it reverberates beyond you. The King's favor and kindness can resonate from generation to generation. But it has to start with somebody.

Why not you?

Elevation Requires an Upgrade

When Phibs is on his way to King David's palace, he has every reason to believe the king wants to destroy him. But the truth is, David wants to *restore* him. Remember the three promises?

1. I will show you kindness.
2. I will give you all your grandpa's property.
3. You will eat with me at the king's table.

Spending time in the king's presence, learning to accept his kindness, begins a transformation inside Phibs. His outward location has changed, but in order for his inward disposition (Lo-debar) to catch up with his changed circumstances, he needs a lot of time in the loving presence of the king. Why is this important? Because King David is going to make Phibs master of everything his grandfather King Saul once owned.

With a snap of David's fingers, Phibs goes from being a borrower to a lender, from being a beggar to a wealthy landowner.

Watch out, y'all. I'm about to preach this thing.

He's got to get Lo-debar out, because now he has livestock that need to be pastured—and "a place with no pasture" mindset ain't gonna cut it. His elevation means that he can't keep everything the same. He can't camp out on Makir's beer-stained sectional and play *Call of Duty* for sixteen hours a day. He can't binge all six seasons of *Empire* (again).

What are you trying to say, Pastor Mike?

God's upgrade calls for your upgrade.

I'm telling you, when grace drops in, *you* can't keep everything the same either. The hard heart work we're doing here is necessary for the next level God has for you.

When God elevates you to become the CEO you've always dreamed you could be, you can't keep insisting you don't like to read. You better renew your mindset, future CEO.

> God's upgrade calls for your upgrade.

Let me just tell on myself.

High school Mike Todd used to say things like "Reading is boring. I'll get the CliffsNotes. I'll rent it at Blockbuster." Lead pastor Mike Todd *loves* to read. If I don't read often and purposefully, I disqualify myself from the position God has elevated me to.

Tell you the truth, lead pastor Mike Todd would still like to say things like "I hate working out. It's hard, and I've got better things to do." But God has told me clearly, "I can bless your ministry only to the degree your body can take it." If I don't strengthen and condition the only body He has given me (His temple), it won't be able to keep up with where He's elevated me.

What disciplines do you need to exercise to match your elevation?

What priorities do you need to change to embrace your platform?

What habits do you need to break to handle your influence?

What mindset do you need to undo to receive God's upgrade?

I'll Take That

According to Google Dictionary, *restore* means "to bring back, to return something or someone to a former condition, place, or position." And restoration is exactly what our King intends for us, no matter the extent of our damage. It's what He intends for *you*.

When grace drops in, God restores generational blessings. What's that? Well, just like Saul had earthly wealth that would have eventually been his grandson's inheritance, God has an abundance of blessings earmarked for your family line: you, your parents, your grandparents, and your ancestors even further back.

Some of y'all are saying, *Where is it at? I sure could use an abundance of blessings right now.* The truth is, all kinds of things can happen to disrupt the passing of generational blessings. Sometimes our forefathers or foremothers weren't obedient, so God's blessing slipped through their fingers. That's what happened in the case of King Saul. But lost blessings aren't always about disobedience. Here's an example that's close to home for me.

My grandmother Leola Jones was a minister of the gospel in the Reisor neighborhood of Shreveport, Louisiana, mostly from her kitchen because she wasn't afforded

> When grace drops in, God restores generational blessings.

an opportunity, whether because of her gender or race or both, to expand any further. She was gifted and called and faithful, and she had an impact on the community around her for the gospel's sake.

Leola passed her mantle of ministry to my mother, Brenda Jones Todd, who answered God's call at twelve years old and has done greater exploits for the kingdom than Leola ever dared to imagine. She has ministered with my father on platforms across the nation and around the world to tens of thousands, maybe hundreds of thousands, in need of Jesus. But not even my mom received everything God had stored up for our family line.

Then, when the mantle of ministry was passed to me, I inherited what I'd call generational blessings, an abundance of blessings. Who gets handed a church that is already paid off and ready and raring to grow? Those weren't *my* blessings. No, I'm convinced that the blessings I began my ministry with were my mom's and grandmother's and possibly my great-grandmother's blessings rippling outward as evidence of God's grace and favor on our family. For various reasons my foremothers couldn't walk fully into those blessings, so when grace dropped into my life, they were restored to me. Not only that—I, in turn, can be faithful to pass those blessings on and trust the Holy Spirit to compound them in and for my children and their children too!

There is a blessing God intended for your dad, grandad, or great-grandad that has been waiting for someone in your family to step up and say, "I'll take that." You might have thought it was lost forever, but God says, "Look at My record. I made a covenant with Abraham that was fulfilled generations later through Joshua, who finally led My people into the Promised Land. The folks Joshua led into Canaan, that land flowing with milk and honey, were the *children* of the slaves Moses led out of Egypt. Just because their parents fumbled the blessing doesn't mean I did. I made good on My word, and their kids received My blessing."

What God has for your family is *for your family,* but somebody has to have enough 𝕮𝖗𝖆𝖟𝖞 𝕱𝖆𝖎𝖙𝖍 to claim it and say, "I'll take that." So let's exercise some faith talk.

Confidence in my identity? I'll take that.

Living a Spirit-empowered life? I'll take that.

Living out my purpose? I'll take that.

A healthy marriage? I'll take that.

Financial stability? I'll take that.

Mental health? I'll take that.

Emotional intelligence? I'll take that.

Children who serve God? I'll take that.

Healthy family relationships? I'll take that.

Safe, growing friendships? I'll take that.

Blessing those around me? I'll take that.

Breaking generational cycles? I'll take that.

Freedom from addiction? I'll take that.

Embracing a rhythm of rest? I'll take that.

Being fruitful and multiplying? I'll take that.

Leaving an inheritance of blessing? I'll take that.

Healing from my damage? I'll take that.

If you haven't got it by now: God's plan for you is restoration.

You might come from generations of divorce, divorce, divorce.

You might have a genetic predisposition to develop breast cancer.

You might be heir to a fortune of mismanaged hopes and dreams.

You might have your daddy's eyes as well as his poverty mentality.

You might come from a long line of anger-management issues.

None of these are what God intended for your family, and they're not what He intends for you. This is what He intends:

Instead of shame and dishonor,
>> you will enjoy a double share of honor.
You will possess a double portion
>>> of prosperity in your land,
>> and everlasting joy will be yours.
(Isaiah 61:7)

These are the King's promises! Don't let your old dead-dog mentality keep you from believing it!

It's okay if you're not 100 percent convinced yet. Phibs isn't at first either. He's got a lot of breakfasts, lunches, and dinners to eat at the king's table of grace before he believes he's anything more than a dead dog destined for nothing but Lo-debar. He'd probably be thrilled if the king put him up at the Holiday Inn with a continental breakfast. Like, *I love me some toaster waffles! Oooh, and Frosted Flakes? Tony the Tiger is my boy.*

But the king has so much more than Eggos in mind for Phibs.

David wants his best friend's son to thrive, not just to survive. Not to beg. Not to make do. To *flourish,* and for Mephibosheth's flourishing to ripple outward as continuous grace into the lives of everyone around him.

Speaking of which . . .

When the King's Blessing Is for Someone Else

Phibs gets elevated, but he's not the only one. Look at this:

> Then the king summoned Saul's servant Ziba and said, "I
> have given your master's grandson everything that be-
> longed to Saul and his family. You and your sons and
> servants are to farm the land for him to produce food for
> your master's household. But Mephibosheth, your master's
> grandson, will eat here at my table." (Ziba had fifteen sons
> and twenty servants.)
>
> Ziba replied, "Yes, my lord the king; I am your servant,
> and I will do all that you have commanded." (2 Samuel
> 9:9–11)

Let's be honest, now. "Yessir" is the only thing Ziba *can*
say. He doesn't have other viable options. David isn't a city
mayor or a state governor or the U.S. president who offers
somebody a job that they can refuse. No. David is the king.
His word is the law that governs the entire land. He says
"Go," and you go. He says "Jump," and you say "How
high?" He says "Run," and you say "How far?" and "Can I
get you anything else, sir?"

Ziba has served two different kings, and he knows what's
up. He knows "I will do all that you have commanded" is the
only answer available to him.

That doesn't mean he's happy about it. As the story goes
on, we'll find out that Ziba is very unhappy indeed.

Instead of rejoicing over Mephibosheth's restoration and
elevation, Ziba gets jealous. From head to toe, he's absolutely
green with envy over the king's favor on Phibs's life. Why
would the king bless this damaged mess of a man, this crip-

pled grandson of an enemy, Saul, who tried to murder him a dozen times in the distant past? (See 1 Samuel 18–26.) It doesn't make any sense!

Here's what we have to understand, though, to really put Ziba's envy in perspective. Remember how it was common practice in ancient times for a new king to execute the whole family of the old king to lessen the chances of a civil war? Well, it wasn't only family members who typically got knocked off. As a rule, the ex-king's entire household, including his servants and their spouses and kids, was taken out *Godfather*-style. That's gangsta.

What does that mean? It means Ziba should be dead. It means grace has dropped into *his* life too. How do we know? Because Ziba is still breathing. Instead of the new king putting a hit out on Saul's entire household, including Ziba and his sons and his servants, David restores them all and lets them participate in his kingdom.

But the king doesn't stop there! He *elevates* Ziba and his family into multigenerational job security. Ziba gets a promotion! The move from back-of-palace servant to property manager of a royal estate is a come-up, the ancient equivalent of working the sales floor and then moving up to the corporate office. But a come-up gets cut short when you start comparing. Instead of comparing the blessing of his new position with where he used to be, Ziba starts looking at Phibs's blessing. It looks to me like Ziba needs to upgrade *his* mindset too.

> **A come-up gets cut short when you start comparing.**

If you are bitterly jealous and there is selfish ambition in your heart, don't cover up the truth with boasting and lying. For jealousy and selfishness are not God's kind of wisdom. Such things are earthly, unspiritual, and demonic. For wherever there is jealousy and selfish ambition, there you will find disorder and evil of every kind. (James 3:14–16)

Jealousy is a gateway sin. When envy takes over your imagination, you eventually find yourself in places you never thought you'd be, doing things you never thought you'd do, chasing things that were never yours to begin with. First jealousy, then selfish ambition, and the next thing you know, you're boasting, lying, manipulating, and up to your eyeballs in evil of every kind.

This is what I call the Ziba Zone.

Stay out of the Ziba Zone.

But how, Pastor Mike?

God wants to restore and elevate you. But He also wants you to rejoice when He restores and elevates other people (Romans 12:15). Oh, you may think they don't deserve it. You may think they're sorry and better off lost in Lo-debar. But hear me when I say this: If you ever find yourself comparing yourself with the Mephibosheths around you, you're missing the whole point. *They* are not who you should be worried about. If their status makes you jealous, you're not paying attention to the person who matters: the King. God. He's the one who is over elevation.

Promotion cometh neither from the east, nor from the west, nor from the south.

But God is the judge: he putteth down one, and setteth up another. (Psalm 75:6–7, KJV)

The king's kindness, the king's generosity, the king's grace, are the only things Ziba should be noticing.

What would be different in your life if you stepped out of the Ziba Zone to notice and give genuine thanks for the restoration and elevation God is doing in other people's lives? I dare you to find someone *this week* to celebrate. When somebody else gets blessed in the coming days, I challenge you to rejoice with them. Don't just scroll by their post or act like you don't hear them sharing how God's grace and favor are dropping like rain. Get excited. Leave a comment. Shout them out. Shoot them a text or DM. If you're feeling real crazy, call them on the phone. Write them a note, or mail them a card through the U.S. Mail, with a stamp and everything. Focus your attention on the grace-filled King who is restoring and elevating damaged people everywhere for His glory.

If He does it for them, He is able to do it for you.

Stay out of the Ziba Zone.

It's more fun to celebrate than it is to hate.

8

WHEN DAMAGE IS AN INSIDE JOB

The Domino Effect of Dysfunction

Every family is a little bit dysfunctional because families are made of people, and people are cracked, broken, and jacked up. Damaged. But let's face it: Some people—and therefore some families—are more dysfunctional than others. Who do you know who comes from a dysfunctional family? If you can't think of anybody, it's probably you. But in all seriousness, if that describes your people, I hope getting to know the drama in Mephibosheth's family (psycho grandpa and murdered dad) is reassuring to you. I know it is for me. Here's the good news: Even family-of-origin damage isn't beyond the King's ability to restore.

Phibs's family isn't the only one with issues in 2 Samuel. In fact, David may be great and good as Israel's king, but he is a deadbeat dad to his own kids. (It just goes to show, the only *real* hero of the Bible is Jesus. Even Bible heroes need Him.) David has unhealed damage of his own—and in his case, the damage becomes a gen-

> Even family-of-origin damage isn't beyond the King's ability to restore.

erational curse instead of a generational blessing. He passes down his damage to the next generation.

Let me give you a trigger warning before I sum up three action-packed chapters of the Bible in five minutes. Second Samuel 13–15 is some scandalous scripture. There is nasty stuff in here. I'm not talking spit-on-your-brother nasty; I'm talking *Game of Thrones* or *The Color Purple* nasty. Y'all don't hear me. I'm talking so nasty it makes *Jerry Springer* look family friendly. I won't get into graphic details, but let's just say an older brother's sexual violation of his little sister is the first domino of a thousand tragic dominoes. So stick with me, if you can stomach it, as I give you an overview of David's dysfunctional and damaged family. It's important if we're going to understand what happens next with Phibs and Ziba.

One of the king's sons, Amnon, lusts after one of the king's daughters, Tamar. (If you're doing the math, that makes them half siblings: same daddy, different mamas.) Instead of taking his temptation to the Lord, alerting accountability, asking for prayer, or even hitting the gym for leg day, Amnon comes up with a scheme to rape her—and then follows through with his evil plan. Not only is Tamar sexually violated, as appalling as that is; she is also socially humiliated and shunned by her community. Through absolutely no fault of her own, Tamar is considered damaged goods from that day on.

No one holds Amnon accountable. The Bible says, "When King David heard what had happened, he was very angry" (2 Samuel 13:21). Well, okay. Anger can be a good place to start if it eventually leads to justice. But the Scriptures tell us that David gets mad, gets over it, and then moves on.

Let's stop right here and let that sink in. Yes, it was a different time and culture—but seriously? I have three beautiful daughters, y'all. If that ever happened, somebody would be getting hands laid on them immediately (to be clear, not for prayer), and I'd be headline news (again). Hear me: I believe in calm, cool, and collected conflict resolution, but when it comes to my babies? I can't make no promises. Keep praying for me—God's not finished with me yet. Any parents out there feel me?

Poor Tamar, who doesn't have the luxury of moving on, takes refuge in the household of one of her other brothers, Absalom. Absalom is furious with Amnon on her behalf. And when he realizes that David—their father, *the king,* who has ultimate power to protect and avenge—isn't going to give justice to Tamar by administering judgment to their rapist half brother, he's filled with rage. Since David does nothing, Absalom hatches a plan to kill Amnon—and another domino falls when he follows through with his evil scheme.

Now get this: No one holds Amnon accountable for rape, and no one holds Absalom accountable for murder. The Bible tells us that David mourns for his son Amnon "many days" while Absalom flees the country. He stays away for three years until "King David, now reconciled to Amnon's death, longed to be reunited with his son Absalom" (2 Samuel 13:39). Absalom lies low in neighboring Geshur and waits for Daddy to get over it and move on.

And eventually Daddy does!

The king allows Absalom to return to Jerusalem, as though none of that unpleasant Tamar-Amnon business ever happened. As if being the king's son means Absalom can literally get away with murder.

I know this seems so outlandish, as if it could never ever happen today. But may I submit to you that many families today allow the domino effect of dysfunction to divide and devastate them every holiday season? Shoot, forget holidays.

There's drama every time the family gets together! Sharp darts—words, actions, environment, and exposure—get hurled at the people we're supposed to love. And inevitably, even though they may not show it, somebody gets damaged. We know there are problems. We know there is pain. We can feel the pressure—but nobody talks about it! It's business as usual, like nothing ever happened.

> **Wounds heal properly only when they are properly treated.**

Sound familiar?

We've believed this notion that time heals all wounds, but that's a lie. Wounds heal properly only when they are properly treated.

The King's Justice

Time goes by, and Absalom knocks down another domino. He hatches another plan—and this one is heavy with irony. He starts by showing up early each day at the city gate, where people come to petition the king for—you guessed it—justice:

> When people brought a case to the king for judgment, Absalom would ask where in Israel they were from, and they would tell him their tribe. Then Absalom would say, "You've really got a strong case here! It's too bad the king doesn't have anyone to hear it. I wish I were the judge. Then everyone could bring their cases to me for judgment, and I would give them justice!"
>
> When people tried to bow before him, Absalom wouldn't

let them. Instead, he took them by the hand and kissed them. Absalom did this with everyone who came to the king for judgment, and so he stole the hearts of all the people of Israel. (2 Samuel 15:2–6)

Do you see the irony? The brother-killer wins the people's hearts by promising the very thing David has failed to deliver in Absalom's own case: *justice*. And on the strength of those promises, the son raises a full-fledged rebellion against his father's reign. Eventually Absalom slips out of the city, gathers an army from every tribe in Israel, then heads back to take the throne for himself.

When David hears that all this is going down, he decides that his only course of action, if he wants to avoid a full-blown civil war, is to leave the city and let the dominoes fall where they may. Maybe Absalom will make a fatal mistake. Maybe the people will turn against his brother-killing, throne-stealing son. But if David chooses to stand against Absalom, the whole nation will be at war with itself.

Who is responsible for this mess?

Certainly not Tamar. She's the only person in this sordid soap opera who is truly a victim (*it wasn't her fault*) and not a perpetrator of damage. Amnon is a good candidate to take the blame. Raping your sister is some next-level wicked Dark Age thuggery. But at the end of the day, Amnon's lust is an aftereffect of an environment of damage. Absalom also isn't anyone's idea of a saint. He throws plenty of his own darts, and at least one of them is deadly. But at the end of the day, Absalom's rage is allowed to escalate unchecked.

The sons' defects are ripple effects of the father's damage. David may think that Absalom is sabotaging him, but the truth is, sabotage is an inside job. It starts silently, hidden inside David long before it ever provokes rebellion in his son. I wonder what David's dartboard of damage looks like.

Did a dart hit kid David in the domain of rejection when his dad didn't bother to invite him to meet the prophet Samuel?

Did a dart hit teenage David in the domain of abuse when King Saul commanded him to play music and then threw spears at him?

Did a dart hit young man David in the domain of accelerated success when the whole nation celebrated his victories over Israel's enemies?

Remember, height doesn't equal healing. David is now king of an entire nation, but the one person who has gone with him everywhere is himself. You take the real you with you wherever you go. His unhealed damage is undermining his family and his reign. Consider how differently David treats Mephibosheth and Tamar. When it comes to his deceased best friend's son, he goes above and beyond to show kindness and offer restoration. When it comes to his own daughter, he drops the ball and doesn't say a word.

> **You take the real you with you wherever you go.**

His damage is a hindrance to both his fatherhood and his kingship—and he doesn't even realize it. How differently things could have turned out if David had done his own work (like the work you're doing now) and received God's healing! I wish he would have prioritized healing and tackled step 3.

1. Remember the hit. (Did that. Check.)
2. Recognize the hurt. (And that. Check.)

3. **Realize the hindrance. (It's time to do this.)**
4. Reset to humility.
5. Receive God's healing.

3. Realize the Hindrance

Take the log out of your eye.

Silent Sabotage

Isn't it funny how easy it is to see the toilet paper stuck on somebody else's shoe? How is it even possible that they don't know? Those three or four bright white squares are a silent billboard announcing exactly where they've been and what they've been doing. They're out here dragging a damp streamer of evidence behind them, and they have no idea.

Sometimes our damage is just like that: easy for everybody else to see and invisible to us. Before we judge King David too harshly, I want to admit that I can relate. I, too, have allowed unhealed damage to become a hindrance—not because I didn't care or because I was being reckless, but because I didn't know. I couldn't see. I didn't realize.

I didn't realize that my obsession with greatness would rob me of everyday joys.

I didn't realize that when I traded good for great, I would miss meaningful moments that I can never get back.

I didn't realize that demanding perfection from others would cut off their opportunity to grow.

I didn't realize that idolizing the ideal would send me into isolation.

My obsession with greatness was an adaptation to damage

(*They never let me play!*) that served me for many years in many settings—until it didn't. Until one day my wife asked, "Why are you like that?" and I realized that *something* (I didn't know what yet) was hindering me from being all that God made me to be. Natalie saw the metaphorical toilet paper snagged on my sneaker and was like, "You need to handle that."

> **I realized my damage was a hindrance to my present and my future.**

It was one of the most significant revelations I have received in this season of my life: I realized my damage was a hindrance to my present and my future. If I remained broken and unhealed, my relationships would be restricted. My destiny could be delayed. My future could be forfeited. My dreams could become nightmares.

Those closest to me could feel disconnected. If I never climbed off the hamster wheel of success, my sanity would be in jeopardy.

Transformation Church has heard me say "Progression, not perfection" approximately 5,487,322 times. (Pretty sure I've now said it at least twice in this book. Maybe three times. Okay, four.) But the truth is, I started saying it to encourage and support other people a *loooooong* time before I believed it for myself. Progress was just fine for everyone else. Of course God didn't expect *you* to be perfect! Progress was good enough for God and other people, but it was greatness or nothing for Mike Todd.

Once I realized how hypocritical that was, I knew it was time to H.U.S.H. I needed to Hear from God, Understand progressively, Share intimately, and get to the Heart of the matter. And the Heart of the matter was that my damage was a hindrance.

A Prototype of Progression

When I was fifteen, my youth pastor, Terrell Taylor, chose me to direct a gospel group of my peers. We called ourselves One Generation of Praise. There were bold, colorful matching outfits, very serious photo shoots, and choreography that would make Usher happy.

We spent four years—in teenage time, that's essentially forever—working on a nineteen-song album we titled *The Prototype*. This record was my life, y'all. My dad helped me turn my bedroom closet into a soundproof vocal booth, and I traded my comfortable bed for a paper-thin futon so we could have a "couch" in the "control room." I spent significant time *every day* for *four years* working to produce and perfect this magnum opus. It felt like the most important thing I would ever do. It was my life's work. So I wanted to get every tweak of reverb, every delay, every EQ exactly right. I was in pursuit of perfection, and I ran hard at it every day.

We sent the final mixes out to be mastered, pressed, and printed, then rehearsed for hours and hours at a time for our big release concert. That was the night *The Prototype* would be launched into the world, and it would go on to sell millions of copies and be beloved by every musician who was important to us. (I didn't say "Grammy," but I sure was thinking it.)

All of us worked so hard. There was plenty of sweat and more than enough tears to go around. We all wanted everything to be perfect.

Well. It wasn't.

You don't have to have watched nineties-era TGIF sitcoms to guess that the big concert was a flop. Problems with the sound plagued us all night and threw us off our musical game, and we just weren't able to replicate live what we'd worked so hard to achieve in the studio. It was a massive disappointment for all of us.

But especially for me.

It wasn't just not good. It was bad.

All that work, four years of my life, for *this*?

A disappointing release concert and less-than-epic album sales negated the value of *The Prototype* project for me. It was immediately irrelevant. I never really listened to it again. For more than a decade, I actively ignored when other people listened to it. If I heard it in another part of the house or at church or in someone's car, I felt embarrassed and ashamed. It took me back to the site of the damage.

This went on for years and years until I had basically erased *The Prototype* from my memory. Fast-forward to a few months ago. Some of my cousins and my little brother Graceson came over to join my Sunday morning workout. We all get down to the gym, and I'm taking music requests to load up a playlist, when my cousin Chelsea shouts, "*The Prototype*!" and everybody goes nuts.

"Yes!"

"Turn it on!"

"That's the one!"

"Play my song—no skips!"

Turns out, *The Prototype* is still a fan favorite.

So in that moment I'm faced with a choice: Shut it down or let it be?

As much as I don't want a seventy-three-minute reminder of my failure, I decide to just go with the flow. To my surprise, the album comes up immediately on Apple Music—so I hit Play to be a good sport and then start stretching to warm up.

Over that next hour-plus, I watch my brother and my cousins sing along at the top of their lungs, harmonizing so easily that I can tell they've listened many (many, many) times. They even pause their reps occasionally to match a particularly intricate vocal run. Their obvious affection and appreciation for something I made so long ago becomes contagious and jumps on my trainer, who starts dancing while putting more weight on the rack. It starts to warm my heart.

But even more unexpected is this: *The Prototype* is good. Like, really good.

The arrangements are solid. The grooves don't quit. The vocals are lush and layered but crystal clear, and there are some genuinely exciting musical moments that I somehow managed to capture in my make-do studio/bedroom closet. Hearing my creative work with fresh ears that day brought to my mind these words of Jesus:

> How can you think of saying to your friend, "Let me help you get rid of that speck in your eye," when you can't see past the log in your own eye? Hypocrite! First get rid of the log in your own eye; then you will see well enough to deal with the speck in your friend's eye. (Matthew 7:4–5)

I realized during that workout that I'd found yet another way my obsession with greatness was a hindrance. I couldn't appreciate my own good work and, more importantly, God's good work through me. Talk about self-sabotage!

If you're like me, self-sabotage isn't your goal—but correcting it is now your job. You're not consciously trying to undermine your relationships, creative pursuits, career, and future success. But now you've got to take responsibility to realize the hindrance.

Realize that passivity will keep you from purpose.

Realize that unforgiveness will keep you from understanding.

Realize that excuses will keep you from executing.

Realize that poor communication will keep you from connection.

Realize that procrastination will keep you from progressing.

Realize that a victim mentality will keep you from seeing victory.

Realize that negative self-talk will keep you from self-love.

Realize that comparison will keep you from community.

Realize that unhealed damage will keep you from destiny.

Be aware, friend: It is reeeeeeeeeally hard to see self-sabotage on your own. The activity below is best done with a trusted, godly friend or small group who knows you well enough to speak loving truth about how your damage hinders you.

In the table on the facing page, in the left-hand column, write down the lies you believe or have believed based on your damage. Once you've exposed the Enemy's lies, write the truth as God sees it in the right-hand column. (I've done a few as examples to get you started—and there is an extra table at the back of the book if you want to keep going.)

THE ENEMY'S LIES	MY CREATOR'S EYES
I'll just keep going until I drop.	Rest is part of God's design for me.
These white lies aren't a big deal.	God made me for honest intimacy.
Everybody has an attitude.	I'm made to manifest the fruit of the Spirit.
I'm not able to confront family conflict.	God's Spirit equips me to speak truth to those I love most.
Anything less than greatness makes me a failure.	God invites me to sit at His table of grace, no matter what.

A domino of dysfunction can start a chain reaction of negative interactions: hateful words, wounding actions, violating exposures, and toxic environments. That's what happens in David's family because he's unable or unwilling to realize how his damage is a hindrance to himself and so many others.

But a domino of healing can also start a revolution of forgiveness, resulting in a lifetime of love, hearts full of harmony, and undeniable unity. My challenge to you is this: Tip the domino in the direction of healing. Don't let your damage be a hindrance.

DAMAGE CONTROL

Conflicting Stories

Let's pick up where Phibs's story intersects with David's again. Years ago, David relied on God's timing to put him on the throne, rather than fighting King Saul to take it. Now, regardless of his shortcomings as a father and a king, he chooses to trust God again, rather than fighting Absalom to keep the throne.

And that's where we find the king and all his household now: running for their lives from Absalom's army. They've made it out of Jerusalem by the skin of their teeth and are just a little ways past the Mount of Olives . . . and guess who shows up.

Ziba!

Good ole Ziba, Mephibosheth's property manager and ranch foreman. Ziba's there with some pack animals loaded up with food and wine for the king and his household. How thoughtful! How timely! That's some good thinking, Ziba.

"Where is Mephibosheth, Saul's grandson?" the king asked him.

"He stayed in Jerusalem," Ziba replied. "He said, 'Today I will get back the kingdom of my grandfather Saul.'"

"In that case," the king told Ziba, "I give you every-thing Mephibosheth owns."

"I bow before you," Ziba replied. "May I always be pleasing to you, my lord the king." (2 Samuel 16:3–4)

Phibs, no! You turned on King David? You bit the hand that fed you? After everything the king has done to bless you, I can't believe this disloyalty and betrayal. You a liar! A cheater! A deceiver! Heartbreaker! (Shout-out to Profyle.)

When I put myself in David's sandals, I honestly find Ziba's story kind of easy to believe. I mean, if your own son has be-trayed you and is trying to overthrow your kingdom, it's probably not shocking that the old king's grandson is trying to do the same. If Absalom, why not Mephibosheth?

Phibs is betraying me too? He'll have to get in line.

David's reaction is to transfer everything Mephibosheth has to Ziba's ownership. (I hope I'd be less hasty and take time to get all the facts, but the king is having a hellacious day and isn't at his best.)

Phibs's version of the story is different from Ziba's, how-ever. According to Phibs's report—which he gives to David upon the king's return to Jerusalem after (spoiler alert!) Absa-lom's death—Ziba left out a few key details and made up a couple more.

Mephibosheth, Saul's grandson, came down from Jerusa-lem to meet the king. He had not cared for his feet, trimmed his beard, or washed his clothes since the day the king left Jerusalem. "Why didn't you come with me, Mephi-bosheth?" the king asked him.

Mephibosheth replied, "My lord the king, my servant Ziba deceived me. I told him, 'Saddle my donkey so I can go with the king.' For as you know I am crippled. Ziba has slandered me by saying that I refused to come." (2 Samuel 19:24–27)

What we've got here is an extreme case of "he said / he said." Their stories are in conflict. The details don't match up. Phibs says Ziba betrayed him. Ziba says Phibs betrayed the king. Which one is telling the truth?

Here's a twist you might not see coming (I didn't): The Bible doesn't say. *What?* I'm serious—God's Word doesn't say straight out which guy is telling the truth and which one is lying his butt off.

When I read this story the first time, I was like, *Did they leave something out? Is my Bible missing some pages? How are they not gonna tell me what's up between Phibs and Ziba?*

But then I did some deeper study and discovered that the narrator is using a technique every great movie director relies on: He's *showing* instead of *telling*. As readers, we're supposed to take a second and even a third look to see what's really going on. It's not spelled out, but everything we need to know is right here in the details.

When we look closer, Phibs *shows* us that he's on step 4 of the healing process.

1. Remember the hit. (Check.)
2. Recognize the hurt. (Check.)
3. Realize the hindrance. (Check.)
4. **Reset to humility. (It's time to do this.)**
5. Receive God's healing.

Do you know what damage control is? It's when the situation is taking a nosedive and you do everything you can to keep it from a crash and burn. Sounds stressful, right? But Phibs doesn't panic.

You don't have to either.

4. Reset to Humility

Take the low road.

I'm a Fool for You

I travel a lot, and on the rare occasion that I'm early for my flight, I love to watch people whose plane is about to leave race to the gate. It's hilarious. If you're flying commercial and you're late, you better run. I mean *run*. It doesn't matter who you are, how much money you make, how much you weigh, how many people you're traveling with, your ethnicity, or the last time you worked out: When those boarding doors are about to close, you better run, Forrest, run! If you care more about looking cute or like you have it all together, you're gonna miss your flight.

> Sometimes it's worth losing your dignity to get to your destination.

Sometimes it's worth losing your dignity to get to your destination. I confess, I have more than once had to lose my cool to make my connection.

Mephibosheth gets this concept.

The first thing to notice about Phibs's condition when the king gets back is that the man stanks. He is funky. He needs a shower and a shave and needs to change his draws. The robes he's got on could stand up by themselves and should be lit on fire far away from everyone who enjoys breathing. You'd think Phibs would make some effort to get himself correct, cleaned up, before going out to meet the king, right? But when we study the cultural norms of that time and place, we discover that his intentional funkiness is showing us how to ride out a storm of potentially damaging circumstances instead of getting pulled under.

Let me explain.

Something about Phibs's situation rings a bell. Something about an emergency palace evacuation . . . Oh, I remember. He went through something exactly like that when he was five, remember? When the person assigned to help him, his babysitter, dropped him instead, damaging his legs for the rest of his life.

And now, years later, there's another palace evacuation situation, and Ziba is the person assigned to help. But according to Phibs, instead of saddling the donkey so his boss could stay close to the king, Ziba walks away from his responsibilities and leaves Phibs behind—trying to damage him again.

At that point, Phibs has a choice. He can let Ziba's actions destroy him and let Lo-debar back into his life. Or he can let all that time he has spent with the king shape his response to a sudden change of circumstances.

How funky he looks (and—let's be honest—smells) when David rides back into town reveals which choice he made.

Have you ever heard the phrase *sackcloth and ashes*? It's common in many cultures to express grief in a physical and obvious way, to mourn both inwardly and outwardly. In Phibs's day, people would show their sorrow by replacing their regular clothing with cheap cloth used to bag and store grain and smearing ashes on their exposed skin and hair. Phibs's funkiness is evidence that he didn't put on party clothes to celebrate the overthrow of David's reign. He didn't pretty himself up to welcome Absalom the insurrectionist to the palace. He deliberately went unwashed and ungroomed to demonstrate where his loyalties lie. He wants everybody, including the rightful king, to know he is #TeamDavid to the bone, ride or die.

It's not a low-risk choice. Think about it: King David's entire royal court—wives, kids, army generals, cooks, stable hands, *everybody*—abandons the palace, and Phibs is left completely alone. He can't get very far without help. The king's servants carried him to the palace, and the palace is where he'll stay unless someone carries him away. And freaking Absalom is coming! The smart play would be to go along to get along with the new guy, to play both sides and try to survive no matter which way this family drama shakes out.

But instead of the smart play, Mephibosheth makes the faithful play. He doesn't care about looking foolish; he cares only about keeping his connection with the king. He gets humble. He takes the low road.

I'll be real with you: This is a hard one for me, but maybe not in the way you'd think. The hardest thing isn't being H.O.T. (humble, open, and transparent) about the stupid, sinful stuff I've done—porn addiction, premarital sex, car insurance fraud, etc.—because I know the Enemy is defeated by the blood of the Lamb (grace) and the word of my testimony (Revelation 12:11). Talking about my failures keeps me accountable and keeps the devil defeated!

What's hard for me is being vulnerable. Looking weak. Saying ouch. I wish I could be strong and proud and cool and still get healed, you know? But it's just not possible. Humility makes space for the Holy Spirit.

As I moved through the checklist toward healing, I remembered the hit (*They never let me play!*), I recognized the hurt, and I realized the hindrance. But if I was ever going to make it to step 5, I needed to H.U.S.H. and reset to humility. I needed to Hear from God, Understand progressively, Share intimately, and get to the Heart of the matter. And the Heart of the matter was that I was a grown man whose damaged inner thirteen-year-old needed a hug from Jesus.

> Humility makes space for the Holy Spirit.

Man, there ain't nothing cool about that. There's no way to spin it and come out looking like a boss.

And that's why my man Phibs is the prototype. Stinky clothes, funky feet, nappy hair, don't care. Nobody but the king matters to him. Only the king's opinion counts.

I want to be like Mephibosheth.

The King Knows Best

When my kids make a mess or a mistake, they run *to* me, not *away from* me. They don't hide. They want Daddy's help. "Daddy, help!" is yelled or whispered or sobbed at least daily in the Todd house, and then I'm handed something stained, sticky, broken, inoperable, or all of the above. My kids are not afraid to tell me when they mess up, and they're not afraid to ask me to fix it. Humility is natural when there's trust, and my children trust me to know best.

Around the same time I realized that my reluctance to be vulnerable was a hindrance, I also realized that I didn't trust

God the way my kids trust me. Instead of running to the Father the minute I got damaged by others or myself, I would try to sort it out on my own and then present Him with a solution. I told myself I was helping God, as if that's possible. Then I saw how Mephibosheth handles himself with King David, and I learned better.

> Ziba has slandered me by saying that I refused to come. But I know that my lord the king is like an angel of God, so do what you think is best. (2 Samuel 19:27)

Wait. What? Why isn't Phibs arguing his case? Why isn't he laying out all the evidence? Why isn't he walking the king, point by point, through all the ways Ziba has damaged him? Because Mephibosheth trusts David. The king has shown himself again and again to be kind, generous, and trustworthy. He has kept each of the promises he made to Phibs that first day in the throne room.

Phibs is humble enough to believe that the king knows best. Are *you* humble enough to believe that our King knows best? I want to be humble enough to believe it all day, every day. The truth is, the more I trust Him, the easier it gets.

He's never failed me yet.

He's never *not* been faithful.

He's never *not* worked it out.

He's never left me hanging.

He's never forsaken me.

He's never neglected me.

He's never abused me.

He's never rejected me.

That deep level of "the King knows best" trust is what I've been practicing lately. When something doesn't go my way,

I'm praying "Lord, You know best" prayers. Even when I don't *feel* it down deep (yet), I'm practicing deep-level trust:

Lord, You know best about my relationship. I trust You.

Lord, You know best about my finances. I trust You.

Lord, You know best about my career. I trust You.

Lord, You know best about my family. I trust You.

Lord, You know best about my influence. I trust You.

Lord, You know best about the timing. I trust You.

Lord, You know best about my future. I trust You.

Now it's your turn. You may not feel it yet, and that's okay. Trust takes practice, and there's no better time to start. (This exercise is also in the back of the book.)

Lord, You know best about _____. I trust You.

Lord, You know best about _____. I trust You.

Lord, You know best about _____. I trust You.

Lord, You know best about _____. I trust You.

Lord, You know best about _____. I trust You.

Lord, You know best about _____. I trust You.

Close to the King

But Mephibosheth goes even a step beyond trust. Look what he says to David next: "You have honored me by allowing me to eat at your own table! What more can I ask? . . . I am content just to have you safely back again" (verses 28, 30).

Let me say this a different way so it's clear to you what Phibs means: "King David, what matters most to me is being close to you. All the other stuff—property, wealth, status— it's just gravy. It's sprinkles on top. It's all great, and I'm truly grateful, but I can live without it. Being in your presence, eating at your table—that's the only thing that matters to me, because that's what changed my life. I just want to be part of your story."

That kind of humility takes my breath away, y'all. Remember what Jesus prays in the Garden of Gethsemane before His arrest? "I want your will to be done, not mine" (Matthew 26:39). The Son doesn't insist on His own way. He seeks to do the will of His Father, to be part of His story. And it takes Him all the way to the cross.

Looking all raggedy and unsuitable for the occasion, Mephibosheth is showing us what it looks like to follow Jesus. It's not about the extra; it's about the intimacy. It's not about the show; it's about the secret place. It's not about what I get; it's about getting to know God.

The greatest reward of bringing your damage to God isn't that He will heal you (although that's pretty amazing). The greatest reward of bringing your damage to God is getting to know your Designer.

> **The greatest reward of bringing your damage to God is getting to know your Designer.**

I promise, this is what you'll discover after significant time living in the King's household and basking in His presence: He is worth more than all of it put together. More than loving family relationships. More than financial security. More than mental and emotional health. More than life-giving intimacy in marriage. More than success and influence. More than purpose.

I honestly believe that all those

blessings and more are what our Designer has in mind for us and that He's ready to pour them out when we are ready to receive them. But I also *know*, after walking with the King for a good while now, that the purpose of those blessings is to draw us deeper into the Source of them all.

10

DESIGNER DAMAGE

It's All About the Name

It's no secret that I'm a sneaker head. I'd be a sneaker head if I worked at the post office; I just happen to be a pastor. There's just something about a fresh pair of Jordan 1's, a crisp pair of Yeezy's, or an exotic pair of LV sneakers. (Rest in peace, Virgil.)

In May 2022, high-end design house Balenciaga introduced damaged versions of its popular Paris sneaker. The original is a souped-up 1960s basketball shoe that comes in high-top, low-top, or slip-on. The damaged versions were available in two levels of distress: "minor scrapes and scratches" or the limited edition "full destroyed." (Guess which was pricier.)

Balenciaga isn't the first high-fashion label to offer damage by design. Gucci's $950 Screener sneaker has been around for four years, but looking at it, you'd swear it's been sitting in the back of a closet for four or five decades. They are broken in.

The "vintage effect" and "aged patina" of those sneakers aren't random. The damage is carefully crafted to achieve exactly what the designer had in mind. The designer's label, the creator's stamp of approval, is what matters. That's what gives Balenciaga's Paris sneaker value. You might be tempted to think you can grab an $8.99 pair of knockoff Chuck Taylor All-Stars, go ham on them with a box knife and a Sharpie, and get the same effect. But when you're done, all you'd have is a ripped-up pair of knockoff Chucks.

What matters most is whose name is on it, because the value is laced up in the name it carries. When you give your life to Christ, you get a new name. His name. The name that is above every name. At that name, every knee will bow and every tongue will confess He is Lord (Philippians 2:9–11). It's the name that makes demons tremble and sicknesses flee. It's the name that speaks peace to storms and calms the sea. It's the name that provides hope and healing to a lost and broken world. It's the name by which all people will be saved.

The name of Jesus.

When Jesus claims you as His own, you wear His name. You're designer, baby! Your value is tied up in the name you carry. Don't ever go on sale. Don't ever cheapen your worth. Don't ever discount your damage. Because the Designer has placed value in you that is greater than anything you've dared to envision.

Beauty may be in the eye of the beholder, but value is the heart of the Creator. What I'm saying to you is this: No matter what you've been through, because of who designed you, the value is still in you.

Let me be clear: I don't believe God causes damage, but I believe He uses it. What happened to me as a thirteen-year-old drummer who wanted to play in big church—He didn't cause it. But receiving His healing for that wound has convinced me that, for our Designer, all damage is usable

The heavy lifting of healing is on Him.

material. He didn't cause the rejection, but through the healing process, He turned my obsession with greatness into obe-
dience and gratefulness.

It's time for us all to take the last step in the healing process.

1. Remember the hit. (Check.)
2. Recognize the hurt. (Check.)
3. Realize the hindrance. (Check.)
4. Reset to humility. (Check.)
5. **Receive God's healing. (Let's go.)**

The first four steps in this process prepare us for the fifth
step, but we can't take this last one ourselves. The work we
are doing opens us up to God's work. But the heavy lifting of
healing is on Him. Healing is a gift, and our heavenly Father
gives good gifts to those who ask (Matthew 7:11).

5. Receive God's Healing

Let the Designer do His job.

Sneaky Deliverance

Complete deliverance can happen in a moment. I've seen ad-
dicts set free in a split second. I've seen terminal diagnoses
turn around after one prayer. I've seen depressed people overcome with joy in worship.

But many times (maybe even most of the time), deliverance
is gradual. It happens over time, under the radar, in the dark,

behind your back when you're not looking. Sometimes you notice it only after the fact, like when you make a different choice than you would have a year ago or when your response to something that used to set you off is surprisingly different. *Something's changed,* you think to yourself. *Oh, wait. It's me.*

I began to notice my deliverance from obsession with greatness when my wife needed me to be present with her through her own journey of healing. We had taken a hit as a family: As I mentioned in chapter 1, our only son, Michael Jr. (MJ), was diagnosed with autism. I canceled six months of speaking engagements like *that* because Natalie needed me and I needed margin to process the hit too.

Making that choice wasn't a hard call, but until then it would have been difficult. That's when I began to discern my deliverance: when I noticed how easy it was for me to choose the good of my family over the great of my platform.

Thank You, Lord, I breathed. *I receive Your healing.*

From my breakfast with Tim Ross at Cracker Barrel to the day I was sure I had received God's healing was about a year of practicing H.U.S.H. During that time, I focused on Hearing from God, Understanding progressively, Sharing intimately, and getting to the Heart of the matter. In worship, in prayer, in conversation with Nat and a small circle of trusted friends, I peeled back layer after layer of damage. I went through the checklist.

I remembered the hit.

I recognized the hurt.

I realized the hindrance.

And I reset to humility.

Then, when I began to consistently choose good over great,

I knew I had experienced God's healing. He was transforming my damage into destiny.

It's more than okay if you're not there yet, my friend. Please don't freak out. Trust the Designer and remember: progression, not perfection. Stay H.O.T. (humble, open, and transparent), and do the work—because that's when and how deliverance sneaks in.

When the Spit Hit the Fan

One way to confirm you're on the path of healing is by seeing what happens when you take a fresh hit.

Remember when the spit hit the fan? (Refresh your memory in chapter 5.) My saliva blew up the internet on Sunday, January 16, 2022, and by Tuesday, I was on a balcony overlooking a vineyard in Napa Valley, H.U.S.H.ing my brains out. It had taken only a couple of hours after the spit clip went viral for me to realize I had to stop hearing from the crowd and start Hearing from Christ. I needed to hear from heaven, not from Instagram—so I needed to go somewhere quiet and turn off my phone. I needed to Share intimately with trustworthy Spirit-filled friends who could Hear God with me and help me Understand progressively what the heck had just happened. So at the last minute, Nat and I joined our best friends, Brie and her husband, Aaron, on a trip they had already planned to Northern California.

What I Heard from God was to pull up a chair to His table of grace and have a bite to eat. So I sat quietly in His presence on that balcony and waited to be fed. I watched workers cutting dry, fruitless brown grapevines. I'd never been to wine country before, and I realized that, in every picture I'd ever seen of a vineyard, it was lushly green and heavy with ripe fruit. I didn't know that tending vines in winter isn't elegant and aesthetically pleasing. They don't put that picture on the brochure. To be honest, it's kind of ugly and even brutal looking, as if they're putting the vines out of their misery.

Sitting there quietly, I Heard the King remind me of His words recorded in John 15:

> I am the true grapevine, and my Father is the gardener. He cuts off every branch of mine that doesn't produce fruit, and he prunes the branches that do bear fruit so they will produce even more. You have already been pruned and purified by the message I have given you. Remain in me, and I will remain in you. For a branch cannot produce fruit if it is severed from the vine, and you cannot be fruitful unless you remain in me. (verses 1–4)

The King was saying to me, "I'm pruning you so that you can produce more fruit. Stay close, and you'll be okay."

What I came to Understand over those few days in Napa was that people's reactions to the spit hitting the fan weren't about me at all—and what God would do with those reactions wasn't about me either. I Understood that the Designer would use all the damage for His glory. What the Enemy had meant for evil, God meant for good—and, thanks to the healing I had already received (*They never let me play—but the value is still in me!*), good enough for God was finally good enough for me.

Sharing intimately with Natalie, Aaron, and Brie helped me excavate the deeper layers of hurt. Tucked away safe with my nearest and dearest, I was able to say how much it hurt to be publicly misunderstood. When we talk and our trusted friends reflect back to us what they've heard us say, our thoughts and feelings go through a kind of distillation or clarification process. My trusted friends' questions brought clarity. Their empathy helped me stay emotionally engaged. Our laughter (so much laughter) brought me back to life. Their sharing of their own journeys helped me feel safe to share even more deeply.

When I got to the Heart of the matter, I discovered that I still cared about the crowd's regard rather than being fully secure in what Christ had called me to do. I had built an idol of people's good opinion, and this very public hit to my reputation was an opportunity to get healed. The last day of our Napa trip, we drove to the beach, which is always a place of spiritual openness for me. Standing there on the sand, cold waves crashing at my feet, I Heard God say, "I created this beach, and you're amazed. But I also created you! Let Me and nobody else define what I have designed."

Damage That Reflects the Designer

The process of healing often takes months or years or decades, especially in the case of childhood trauma. But it can take only days or even hours, once we get in the habit of healing. That was my experience when the spit hit the fan. Because of what I had learned through healing my teenage rejection and disappointment, I already was prepared for the process. It didn't make it easier, but I knew what to expect.

Whatever amount of time it takes, the pattern is the same. By remembering the hit, recognizing the hurt, realizing the hindrance, and resetting to humility, we open ourselves to receive God's healing. Let me break down the process so you can see how the pattern played out in my life in January 2022:

1. **It was easy to remember the hit** because it was fresh.
2. **I recognized the hurt immediately.** It hurt that people I considered friends distanced themselves from me without a conversation. It hurt that my family (especially my brother Brentom) was criticized. It hurt that some critics used the video clip to "prove" something they assumed they knew about me. It hurt that all the good that Transformation Church does in our community and the world was overshadowed in a moment. That whole "sticks and stones may break my bones, but words can never hurt me" thing? Utter nonsense. Words are darts that can cause excruciating damage.
3. **I realized my reaction could be a hindrance.** Back in fourth grade when Freaking Derek was harassing my big brother, I discovered my words have power—and that power can be used for good or for evil, like Dr. Jekyll and Mr. Hyde. (Y'all remember that? In that story, Dr. Jekyll invents a potion to help him get in touch with his darkest desires. He transforms into Mr. Hyde, and bad things happen.) I knew if there was venom in my heart, it would come out in my words—infecting instead of affecting the people I'm supposed to help. Giving in to my darker impulses toward defensiveness and lashing out wouldn't help anyone. I needed to shut down Mr. Hyde and become Mr. Heal, focusing on how to use my words for good.

4. **I reset to humility** and posted a video apology. I didn't defend myself. I ran to God, which felt like running away—Enneagram Eight "The Challenger" doesn't like to run away, so that was humbling. I got vulnerable. I submitted to Nat's insistence that I stay off social media for two weeks. I went back to my assignment, which was preaching a series called "Here Is Holy" (how ironic!) at Transformation Church. It was either humble myself for healing under the mighty hand of God or *be* humbled by my ignorance. All I could hear was Minister Kendrick Lamar saying, "Sit down. . . . Be humble."*

5. By the time I walked into church the next Sunday, I knew **I had begun receiving God's healing.** It was confirmed in an unexpected way. Just before I walked out to preach, my big-little brother Brentom (he's younger but bigger) wrapped me in a bear hug, which prompted me to do something I had never done before: break down in tears. Sobbing in his arms. Y'all, I ugly cried, gasping for breath, out of sheer gratefulness and relief. My response was the epitome of vulnerability and the exact opposite of what I would have done if I were still in an un-healthy space. That's when I knew I was safe. I was whole. I was healing.

Sixteenth-century artisans in Italy invented what came to be known as Venetian mirrors. These intricate works of art are made entirely of glass, including the frames, which are painstakingly attached with tiny handmade screws to a large

* Kendrick Lamar, "Humble," *Damn*, Top Dawg Entertainment, 2017.

center pane of reflective glass. Every exposed surface of a Venetian mirror is reflective. So instead of only one reflection, a Venetian mirror reflects several slightly different angles, giving a more complete picture of the subject standing before the glass.

Most Venetian mirrors today aren't made in Italy, however. They are Venetian in style, made by craftspeople in China or India or elsewhere. Here's what's cool, though. One of the main ways experts evaluate whether or not a mirror is a real antique Venetian is by looking at its damage. Over time, even mirrored surfaces that started out flawless begin to bubble, darken, and crack. So if a Venetian mirror shows very little or no damage, it's highly unlikely that it's genuine. If, on the other hand, a Venetian mirror is dark around the edges or slightly wavy in the center, with the frame chipped or cracked, an appraiser knows that the damage is an indication of authenticity. The damage is evidence of value. The hits, the chips, the cracks—the damage—prove that the artwork is what it claims to be: a handcrafted, one-of-a-kind design by an artist in Venice, Italy.

My dartboard of damage is going to take more hits as time goes on. My boy the apostle Paul tells me to "hold up the shield of faith to stop the fiery arrows [or darts] of the devil" (Ephesians 6:16). Our enemy, the devil, "prowls around like a roaring lion, looking for someone to devour" (1 Peter 5:8), and I hope I'm on his hit list because that means I'm doing something he don't like. The plan is to rob hell.

Hits happen. They're going to happen to me. They're going to happen to you.

My prayer is that the tools I've transparently shared in this book will help you H.U.S.H. and allow Jesus, the Healer, to deal with your damage. If you Hear from God, Understand progressively, and Share intimately, you can get to the Heart of the matter. And the Heart of the matter is that you belong at the table of the King. Every surface, every facet, every flaw, will show the world who made you.

Yeah, you're damaged, but you're not destroyed.

The value is still in you.

THE HEALING KEEPS COMING

Healing is rarely a pretty or straightforward process. Steps need to be repeated, truths need to be practiced, and sometimes we discover other wounds as we move closer to the Heart of the matter. All of that is normal. Remember, healing is not about looking good but about getting into the presence of the King.

The Equation of Damage

Learning this equation has radically changed my life and the lives of those around me. If you do your own work in this section, it will transform you too. This is what the equation of damage looks like:

dart + domain = damage

Let me show you an example:

"You're stupid." + abuse = insecurity
(DART: WORD)   (DOMAIN)   (DAMAGE)

Now it's your turn. Quiet yourself, find a comfortable spot, and use your imagination to go back and visit Little You.

1. **Remember** the first time you experienced disappointment, rejection, abuse, neglect, or one of the other domains of damage. (The full list is on pages 36–37.) What was the domain of your hit?
2. **Identify** what dart was used. Was it words? Was it an action? Exposure? A toxic environment?
3. **Explain** in a word or two how this wound shows up in your life today. This is the step where you have to be H.O.T. (humble, open, and transparent).

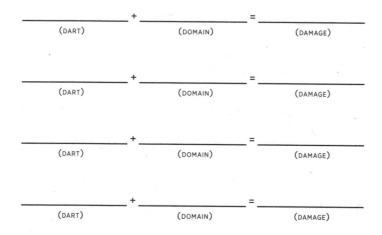

| _____ | + | _____ | = | _____ |
| (DART) | | (DOMAIN) | | (DAMAGE) |

| _____ | + | _____ | = | _____ |
| (DART) | | (DOMAIN) | | (DAMAGE) |

| _____ | + | _____ | = | _____ |
| (DART) | | (DOMAIN) | | (DAMAGE) |

| _____ | + | _____ | = | _____ |
| (DART) | | (DOMAIN) | | (DAMAGE) |

The Dashboard of Damage

Let's get acquainted with our God-designed dashboard. Each gauge on the facing page shows a pair of opposite impulses, habits, or attitudes that indicate damage under the hood. Ideally, when we're letting our healing take the lead, we will sit somewhere in the healthy middle. But when we're driven by our damage, each of us goes to an unhealthy extreme, and those extremes signal when we need a tune-up.

So, where do you go under pressure? Take a few minutes to look at your dashboard. Get quiet and breathe deeply. On each of the gauges below, draw your personal indicator.

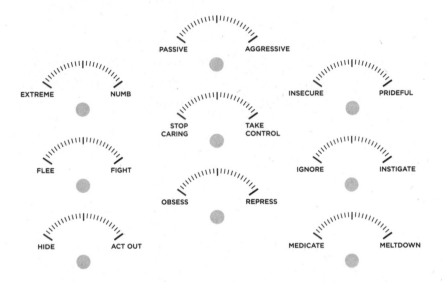

Now that you've taken a good look at your damage indicators, consider and pray about how you might ask for help in moving toward health.

The King's Table

When you need to replace dead-dog feelings, use these pages to remember again that you are welcome at the King's table of grace.

In the space on the next page, write down or sketch out

what's weighing heaviest on your mind or heart right now—especially about yourself. What messages, thoughts, or feelings are keeping you from feeling welcome at the King's table? Be specific and descriptive.

Now let's replace that old way of thinking. Go to page 173 again, and cut out the other blank box. Tape that clean sheet over what you just wrote or sketched. Decorate this new cover with images, words, or verses of Scripture that remind you of God's endless grace.

Whenever you need a reminder of the grace that is always and forever available to you, revisit this page to Hear from God.

The table of grace is set for you. Pull up a chair.

Your "Before" Pictures

An important step toward healing is to take a snapshot of your current condition. We need to be *real* for our "before" picture. No filter. We need to take an inventory of everywhere it hurt.

In the picture frames below, sketch or write about your emotional, mental, spiritual, and/or physical hurts from damage in the past. Include the word *ouch* in at least one, because sometimes you just have to say it.

Yes, recognizing where you're hurt is painful. This level of self-awareness is hard, but I'm believing that your "after" picture is going to make all the work you're doing, with the help of the Holy Spirit, so worth it.

When you recognize the hurt, you make space for grace.

Realizing the Hindrance of My Damage

Be aware, friend: It is really hard to see self-sabotage on your own. This activity is best done with a trusted, godly friend or small group who knows you well enough to speak loving truth about how your damage hinders you.

In the left-hand column below, write down the lies you believe or have believed based on your damage. Once you've exposed the Enemy's lies, write the truth as God sees it in the right-hand column. (I've done one as an example to get you started.) Refer back to the Creator's truth whenever you feel the tug of the Enemy's lies.

THE ENEMY'S LIES	MY CREATOR'S EYES
I'll just keep going until I drop.	Rest is part of God's design for me.

THE ENEMY'S LIES	MY CREATOR'S EYES

Lord, You Know Best

When life doesn't go our way, we can pray our "Lord, You know best" prayers. Even when we don't *feel* it down deep (yet), we can practice deep-level trust.

Are *you* humble enough to believe that our King is this trustworthy? Like our friend Phibs, let's be humble enough to believe all day, every day that the King knows best. The truth is, the more we trust Him, the easier it gets. Let me get you started:

Lord, You know best about my relationship. I trust You.

Lord, You know best about my future. I trust You.

Now it's your turn. You may not feel it yet, and that's okay. Trust takes practice, and there's no better time to start than right now.

Lord, You know best about _____. I trust You.

Lord, You know best about _____. I trust You.

Lord, You know best about _____. I trust You.

Lord, You know best about _____. I trust You.

Lord, You know best about _____. I trust You.

Lord, You know best about _____. I trust You.

Lord, You know best about _____. I trust You.

Lord, You know best about _____. I trust You.

What the Bible Says About Who You Are

If you're in need of some straight-from-God's-mouth validation that the value is still in you, here are some Bible passages to chew on. You can look them up in a physical Bible if you have one, with a Bible app like YouVersion, or even by searching online.

- Romans 8:29
- 2 Corinthians 5:17
- 1 Peter 2:9
- Galatians 2:20
- Ephesians 2:10
- Jeremiah 1:5
- John 15:15
- Colossians 3:3
- Romans 6:6
- Philippians 3:20
- 1 John 3:1
- Psalm 139:14
- Hebrews 4:16
- Matthew 5:14
- 2 Timothy 1:9
- Isaiah 43:4

ACKNOWLEDGMENTS

Every accomplishment in my life has been supported in love and prayer by some very important people, and this is no exception. I have been blessed to be surrounded by a host of people who uplift, execute, and believe in the vision that God has given to me. I would like to take this time to acknowledge my community, my team, my family.

To my wife and so much more, Natalie Diane Todd, your love for me is inconceivable. Thank you for never giving up on me through my deficiencies, insecurity, and immaturity. Your prayers, grace, and patience have allowed me to grow into the man I am today. Thank you for our children, Isabella, Michael Jr., Ava, and Gia—they bring so much bliss into my life. You affirm me and encourage me; you push me beyond my comprehension of success. You will forever be my partner, my passion, and my purpose.

To my parents, Tommy aka "The Captain" and Brenda Todd, thank you for your abounding wisdom and relentless belief in me. Your encouragement, prayers, and examples of faith have shaped me into the man I am today. Thank you for showing me how to lead my family with unconditional love, abundant grace, and strength. Thank you for being the greatest depiction of our heavenly Father's love here on this earth.

To Brie and Aaron Davis, the friends-turned-sister/brother

I never knew was possible, thank you for always being right by my side. Thank you for your persistent authenticity in our friendship. Through every failed project and successful venture, you both have remained a consistent support system. Thank you for taking this journey with me and being everything I've ever needed you to be. And thank you for letting me use your house as my personal "book writing office."

To Charles Metcalf, one of my best friends, a creative samurai, and a sermon-execution specialist, thank you for listening to all my crazy ideas and believing in them at first mention. You give me the space to dream and see visions that are bigger than our current borders. I feel safe trusting you with the raw, unedited, unpolished versions of me, and I pray that every leader gets a Charles Metcalf.

To Jonathan Vinnett, thank you for illustrating the visions of my heart with such clarity. For years, you have made my words come to life and illuminated the ideas that I sometimes couldn't adequately articulate. Your ability to see beyond the tangible has afforded me the privilege to create in the confidence that my vision would be accurately interpreted to the world. Thank you for growing with me on this ever-evolving journey of creativity.

To Alex Field, my literary agent, thank you for playing an instrumental role in making this dream come true. Thank you for your guidance, support, and confidence during the process of this project. You've been by my side every step of the way sharing your wisdom and lending encouragement whenever necessary. Thank you for believing in the vision that was given to me. Thank you for believing in me.

To Aly Hawkins and Channing McBride, thank you for your many contributions to this project. Without you, this would not be possible. Your competence in the literary sphere has ensured that this book would be created and interpreted in excellence. Thank you for taking the time to share this experience with me, helping to organize my many thoughts.

To the team at WaterBrook, thank you for your commitment to the execution and completion of this project. The joy, excitement, and energy that you all brought made this an unforgettably enjoyable experience. Your attention to detail and focus on even the smallest things left me confident that I was working with the right team. All your hard work and efforts are very much appreciated.

To Transformation Church and TC Nation, this is for you! Thank you for your love, support, and prayers for me and my family. The relentless affection that I feel from you motivates me to continue fulfilling my purpose. To the TC Staff, thank you all for your continued dedication and commitment to the vision and partners of TC. Thank you for allowing me to represent God outside the walls of our church. I'm humbled and honored to be your leader.

ABOUT THE AUTHOR

MICHAEL TODD is the lead pastor of Transformation Church in Tulsa, Oklahoma, alongside his wife, Natalie. They were entrusted with Transformation Church by the founding pastor, Bishop Gary McIntosh, in 2015, after fifteen years of leadership.

Their personal philosophy and driving passion at Transformation Church is re-presenting God to the lost and found for transformation in Christ. They aspire to reach their community, city, and world with the gospel presented in a relevant and progressive way. You can find out more about Transformation Church at www.transformchurch.us.

Todd is also the multiple *New York Times* bestselling author of *Relationship Goals* and *Crazy Faith,* and each year he speaks at influential churches and conferences, such as Elevation Church, VOUSCon, XO Marriage Conference, Gateway Church, and others. Michael and Natalie have been married since 2010 and live in Tulsa with their four children: Isabella Monet, Michael Jr., Ava Rae, and Gia Joy.

You can find out more at
@iammiketodd
and
www.iammiketodd.com.

What Are Your Relationship Goals?!

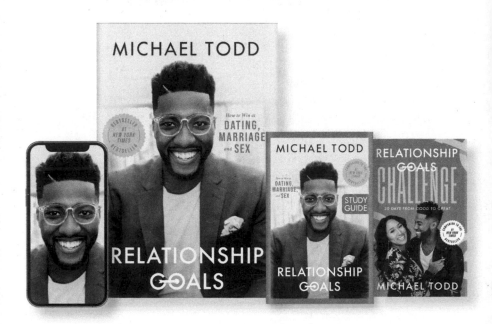

Take your relationship from good to great with *Relationship Goals* by bestselling author Michael Todd. The book plus the *Study Guide* and thirty-day *Challenge* are helping hundreds of couples around the globe win in their relationships!

Prefer to listen and learn?
Get the *Relationship Goals* audiobook
on your favorite audio app!

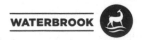

What If You Dared to Believe God for the Impossible?

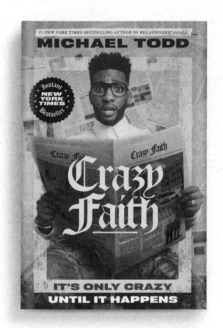

When your prayers seem impossible, holding on to hope requires crazy faith!

Learn how to step out in faith with the life lessons and practical teaching in Michael Todd's *New York Times* bestselling book *Crazy Faith*.

"Michael Todd is the perfect guide to jump-start your faith."
—Craig Groeschel, pastor of Life.Church and *New York Times* bestselling author

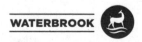